7

11

Start & Run a Home Staging Business

Dana J. Smithers

Self-Counsel Press
(a division of)
International Self-Counsel Press Ltd.
USA   Canada

Self-Counsel Press acknowledges the financial support of the Government of Canada through the Canada Book Fund (CBF) for our publishing activities.

Printed in Canada.

First edition: 2011

Library and Archives Canada Cataloguing in Publication

Smithers, Dana J.
    Start & run a home staging business / Dana J. Smithers.

    ISBN 978-1-77040-055-9

    1. Home staging. 2. Interior decoration. 3. New business enterprises — Management. I. Title.
HD1379.S653 2010   333.33'8068   C2010-902053-7

Cover and inside images
Copyright©iStockphoto/Vase of color/juuce

MIX
Paper from
responsible sources
FSC® C004071

Self-Counsel Press
(a division of)
International Self-Counsel Press Ltd.

1704 North State Street
Bellingham, WA 98225
USA

1481 Charlotte Road
North Vancouver, BC V7J 1H1
Canada

Contents

17 The Stage Is Set

Samples

Forms

Exercises

Acknowledgments

I would like to thank all of my teachers, students, and clients who have taught me so much about starting and running a home staging business. I know they made a difference in my life as I know I made a difference in their lives.

This book is dedicated to my husband who continues to support and encourage me to live out my dreams.

Notice to Readers

Laws are constantly changing. Every effort is made to keep this publication as current as possible. However, the author, the publisher, and the vendor of this book make no representations or warranties regarding the outcome or the use to which the information in this book is put and are not assuming any liability for any claims, losses, or damages arising out of the use of this book. The reader should not rely on the author or the publisher of this book for any professional advice. Please be sure that you have the most recent edition.

Note: Prices, commissions, fees, and other costs mentioned in the text or shown in samples in this book probably do not reflect real costs where you live. Inflation and other factors, including geography, can cause the costs you might encounter to be much higher or even much lower than those we show. The dollar amounts shown are simply intended as representative examples.

Introduction

This home staging business book is written for entrepreneurs just starting out, and for experienced home stagers who want to refresh their business knowledge. The focus of this book is on *how* to start and run a profitable home staging business, although the information could be used by anyone in a design-related industry. It does not cover the physical aspects of staging a property.

The book takes a step-by-step approach to answer the why, how, where, when, and what of starting and running your home staging business. There is an opportunity for you to really take a look at why you want to have your own home staging business and to set goals that will propel you forward. By having a road map for your business you are more likely to succeed than having no idea of *what* you are trying to achieve.

The accompanying CD provides you with home staging forms and exercises to ensure your success as a home stager. You can change the forms in any way you want to suit your needs best — mix and match or use as is with your branding inserted.

Home staging makes a great part-time or full-time business opportunity. You may find as you grow your business that you will need to hire employees, but most likely in the beginning you will work with reliable contractors, and some may even be other home stagers in your area.

If you want to really expand your home staging business, you may decide to invest in some significant rental inventory (such as furniture). You can still create a very lucrative staging business by providing your own small inventory and renting from rental furnishing stores in your area. If you do not have any rental stores in your area, you may have to purchase your own inventory, or you may decide not to work with properties that require larger inventory.

Many savvy sellers over the years have been preparing their property to get it ready for market; in essence, they were doing some home staging. Home staging as a professional service industry began in the mid-1980s in the United States and United Kingdom. It has gradually emerged to become a well-recognized profession throughout Canada as well. Each year the demand for home stagers increases. Staging is now a *must-have* marketing tool for successful realtors and sellers.

Many people do not understand what services home stagers can provide for them. The purpose of staging is to *create broad buyer appeal for the seller's target market* so that the property sells for top dollar and in the quickest possible time. Home stagers do this by offering services such as consultations, report recommendations, shopping services, sourcing for rentals services, installation services, hands-on staging, photography services, and professional organizing. Depending on the skills you already have, you may also be able to confidently add project management and home renovations to your business model. You can create a niche market providing the home staging services you want to offer in your area.

Home staging is a relatively inexpensive start-up business. Unless you are providing significant inventory and need to rent a warehouse, your staging business will more than likely be home-office based. You may incur

a nominal rental cost if you decide to rent a small storage locker. Initially your biggest expense will be spent on your marketing tools such as creating your website and promotional materials. However, this book will introduce you to economical ways to get started with marketing your new business.

You do not need to have a background in interior design to become a successful home stager; if you have completed some interior decorating courses, professional organizing, or other industry-related training, these can be assets but are not necessary. You can be taught the business aspect of starting and running your business, which is the intention of this book.

Having taught and mentored hundreds of home stagers since 2004, I have found that the most successful home stagers have been born with the "gift" of knowing what looks great. Many closet home stagers have been helping their friends and families for years without being paid for their work.

Regardless of whether you are looking for a part-time or full-time career in home staging, this book will give you enough insight into running and operating your home staging business. It will help you determine if this is something you will feel confident doing. It is a fun and creative business to be in if it is the right one for you!

1
Getting Started

As you have probably noticed, there are many popular television shows on home staging. The people on these shows make it look so easy and they always have so much fun! If you think this is what home staging is all about, you are partly right. There is nothing more satisfying than making a room or an entire property look beautiful and having satisfied clients rave about your work. It's equally as satisfying to know that your business reputation is growing because referrals begin to come your way. At that stage, you will feel like you are a successful home staging entrepreneur! However, getting to that stage in your business starts with having the right skills, talents, and attributes.

1. Determining If This Is the Right Business for You

Knowing that this is the right business for you is a necessary component to getting started and will ultimately lead to your success. Asking yourself some key questions before you get

started is the smart thing to do before jumping into something you are not sure is right for you.

1.1 Creative talents and physical abilities

You will need a variety of creative talents and physical abilities to become an expert home stager. Your main objective is to have the creative ability to stage a home so that it has the *WOW!* factor by —

- arranging the seller's own home furnishings (lovely or not) into attractive furniture arrangements, and art and accessory groupings;

- mixing some of the seller's home furnishings with some of your inventory;

- selecting the right rental inventory for a vacant home;

- having the physical stamina to do the labor involved with lifting and carrying furniture and/or by moving product in and out of the home and up and down the stairs, and

- ✔ a passion for creating beautiful spaces that will have broad buyer appeal for the seller's target market, and not necessarily according to your own personal taste

1.2 Skills and attributes

Some of the skills and attributes you will need to have as a great home stager include:

- ✔ Business knowledge on how to start and run a home staging business

- ✔ Professional appearance to attract the type of clientele you want to create long-term relationships with

- ✔ Ability to sell your services as *value-based* whether you are providing product or not

- ✔ Great people skills that allow you to work well with homeowners, realtors, industry-related personnel, and anyone you choose to hire as contractors

- ✔ The ability to present your services in a confident manner, whether during one-on-one meetings with realtors or homeowners, or for groups at trade shows, library talks, and realtor meetings

- ✔ Networking skills that allow you to get connected with like-minded business-people to market your services

- ✔ Ability to be flexible when things go wrong, and problem solve in a timely manner

- ✔ Keen interest in staying on top of your industry through awareness of your colleagues, real estate trends, memberships, meetings, social media, reading, and/or attending conferences

While you may have many of the skills, talents, and attributes listed above, there are a few other things to consider before starting your home staging business. You want to consider if there is a viable market in your area to support your home staging business part time or full time, depending on your goal. Will you have the time, money, and energy to dedicate to your start-up? In the beginning, you will be wearing a lot of different hats and need to be able to take one hat off and put on another until you can afford to hire out work you no longer want to do. How easily can you do that?

Being a home staging entrepreneur can be a very rewarding and fulfilling career choice. It can be a fun business to be in and at the same time it can be a very demanding business to enter into. You will also be working with home sellers who have a lot of different emotions about selling their homes. Some are happy and some are sad; some are upsizing while others are downsizing; some are getting divorced, some are getting married, and some are widowed; some are putting their parents into retirement or care homes; and on the list goes. There will also be some realtors that you click with and establish great relationships with and other realtors that you might want to refer another home stager to work with.

Because home staging is still considered a new service industry, you can be part of this exciting, growing, and emerging industry, if you decide it is the right fit for you! See Exercise 1 to help you assess your home staging skills. The form is also included on the CD.

If you are going to become a home stager, then the answer to most of these questions should be "Yes." If you have some questions you responded "No" to, take a look at those and be honest with yourself. How could you turn them into "Yes"?

EXERCISE 1
SELF-ASSESSMENT FOR HOME STAGERS

No.	Question	Yes	No
1.	Do you watch home staging and home decorating television shows and read home decorating magazines?		
2.	Do friends and relatives always turn to you to help them make their home look great for living and/or selling?		
3.	Do you instinctively know what looks good and what looks bad in terms of decorating?		
4.	Are you physically able to lift furniture and move furniture around?		
5.	Do you currently organize your time well and set goals for yourself?		
6.	Are you a great multitasker who can wear many hats?		
7.	Do you enjoy working on your own some of the time and with others some of the time?		
8.	Whether you have had a business before or not, do you think you can learn what you need to know to start and run a successful business?		
9.	If you need help, will you call on a professional to assist you?		
10.	Is there someone you know who could be your assistant when you need help for the hands-on staging?		
11.	Do you have a support team that will cheer you on and help you celebrate every success?		
12.	Once you know your business well, will you be able to sell your services and/or product easily?		

2. Setting Your Goals

Prior to deciding to start your own home staging business, you probably had some ideas about how you would go about starting your business. You may have a vague idea of what you wanted to achieve and how you would go about doing it. You may have only looked as far ahead as the current or next year, or you may have done a substantial five-year formal business plan that you could take to the bank to get financial support. If you are going this route, it is most likely that you are going to have a warehouse of inventory for your start-up. If you are not, you will be doing what is called a "road map" or an informal business plan. No matter what your style is, you do need to have a business plan that meets your goals. (See Chapter 2 for details on creating a business plan.)

Goal setting is a critical part of today's entrepreneurs' successes. I suggest that if you are unfamiliar with setting goals for yourself that you start doing this on a daily basis. You may already be doing this in the form of your daily to-do list. This is a type of goal setting. You might be someone who loves making that check mark once you accomplish your goals. I am!

2.1 SMART goals

Many years ago when I was taking sales training, I was introduced to the SMART goals method. I have used it for years and recommend that you become familiar with it. It is the only way you can turn your dream into a reality. Dreams must be time and action bound otherwise they stay in the ether and never materialize for you!

I would like to give you a heads-up on how you might be feeling when you are just starting your home staging business:

- Overwhelmed
- Unbalanced by the "idea avalanche" in your head

- Doubtful that you can do all that you want to
- Fearful of making mistakes

There is a way to avoid these negative feelings and turn them into positive ones. Take baby steps in setting your goals. Incorporate the SMART goal setting method on a daily, weekly, monthly, and yearly basis:

S — Specific: Keep your goal small and simple; you can build on this.

M — Measurable: Determine the criteria you will use to ensure you can measure how much of your goal you have accomplished.

A — Achievable: Set the goal so that you can achieve it.

R — Realistic: Evaluate if the goal is achievable in the time and manner you are suggesting.

T — Time bound: This is what gives structure to your goal; you will know if you have accomplished your goal or not if you achieve it within the time frame you set.

Once you become familiar with using this SMART method and goal setting you will be able to write your business plan with confidence.

2.2 Determine your revenue streams

One of the most important concerns that the majority of new entrepreneurs have is determining how much money they *need* to make. I use the word "need" because you will want to be realistic in determining what your sales will be as well as your operating costs, especially in your first year of business. (For more on operating costs, see Chapter 9.) I highly recommend that you work your sales figures backwards, deciding how much money you need to make, and then determine what home staging services you will offer that will allow you to make the sales revenues you are projecting.

Depending on your financial situation, you may be able to start working on your home staging business right away with no concern of bringing in an income. However, if you need to stay in the job you currently have, start making plans to reduce the number of hours you work at your job or look for a more flexible job, which will give you time to start working on your own home staging business.

If you decide to look for part-time work, then I recommend you look for work in a related field. If your passion is lighting, then apply to work part time in a lighting store. If you love paint and color, consider applying at a paint store. Perhaps working with a mortgage broker is a better fit. Go where your passion takes you and where you can start to build your strategic alliances while learning about other businesses related to the home staging industry. If you live in an area where there are home staging businesses, see if you can work part time for one or some of them. You may be required to have insurance if you work for a home staging business as a contractor. (See Chapter 5 for more information on insurance.)

A fun exercise to do is to look at where 100 percent of your revenues are going to come from. Sample 1 shows what your revenue streams might be if you started part time. On the CD you will find a blank chart called "Your Revenue Streams" to use when figuring out your own revenue streams.

Often your first year can require that you do whatever it takes to get your business going. Everyone's financial situation will be different and, therefore, their approaches will be different as well. This is a guide for you to use to work backwards, to grasp where you see yourself in year one, year two, year three, etc. Once you start your business, you will be continually reassessing what your business *is* and the goals you have set. Your goals will be based on what income you *need* to maintain and grow a successful business.

SAMPLE 1
REVENUE STREAMS

100% Revenues — Year One		
Part-time job 75%	Part-time staging 15%	Other: Commissions from decorating stores 10%
100% Revenues — Year Two		
Part-time staging 50%	Part-time retail 25%	Other: Commissions, referrals 25%
100% Revenues — Year Three		
Staging 75%	Other: Commissions, referral fees, product sales 25%	

2
Developing Your Business Plan

One of the first steps in starting your business is to develop your business plan. This way, you are creating a road map that allows you to know where you are going and what you need to do to get to where you want to be in your business. Most home stagers do an *informal* business plan, which contains many of the same components as a *formal* business plan.

A more formal business plan is necessary if you want to borrow money from a bank or private investor. In the formal business plan, more time and energy will be spent on gathering information about your financial forecast and risk management.

When you are writing your formal business plan it is highly recommended that you work with an accountant and lawyer to assist with it. Check to see if there are any government agencies in your area who offer this service for free, or at a minimal cost to you.

Your business plan is a terrific tool that is worthy of the time it takes to create. It is your road map to success whether you are looking for lenders or not. By having a good solid business plan you can see where you are going and you can measure your success with it.

1. What Goes into the Business Plan

Whether you decide to go the route of a formal or informal business plan the following sections cover the criteria that you will need for both. Much of the information required for your business plan is discussed in more detail in later chapters so you may want to read the whole book before you prepare your business plan.

As you start to grow your business you will be checking in with your initial business plan to see if you are on track or not. If you are not on track, you may need to seek professional advice to see what you need to do to get your business back on track.

Business coaches play invaluable roles in start-up businesses, so this is something you might want to consider. There are also mentors in home staging who would be able to assist you with meeting your targets.

1.1 Executive summary

The executive summary is the introduction to your business and an overview of what will be discussed in your business plan. Typically, the summary is no more than a page long. It will contain the highlights of your business plan including your business venture, competitive advantage, and your bottom-line needs to start the business. If you are looking for a bank loan or a private investor, they like to read this part first.

The executive summary is the first thing readers will see, but it is the last section you will write. This section summarizes the key points of your entire business plan.

1.2 Defining your vision and mission statements

Before you purchased this book you had some idea about what you wanted your future to look like. Most people start with a dream and then set goals with action steps to make their dreams become realities. By creating your vision you can be more focused on what you want your reality to look like. One of the first steps in deciding what your vision will look like is to start writing down your ideas of what you want your business to achieve. Make it very "big picture" thinking; the details (i.e., the how to) come later.

I recommend that you find some quiet time and sit with pen and paper in hand and just start "green light" thinking in which you do not censor any idea that comes to you. It does not matter how foolish or crazy an idea may seem to you. Write it down because once you see it in print, you have "put it out there" and solidified the "what" of your dream. You can delete later!

Exercise 2 will help you with your green light thinking. You can print out a copy from the CD for this exercise.

Once you have done Exercise 2, take a break and then come back to your list and circle the ideas that you think could actually work for you. This is still green light thinking, but with a reality check. Trust your intuition and see how each idea settles with you. Does it bring you joy? Or does it feel heavy? Is the goal a bit too big for right now? You are looking for the words that feel joyful to you. From this list of ideas you have circled, write your vision of what your business will look like. Your vision might be something like this:

I have my own successful home staging business with the most fabulous clients. My life is balanced so that I work 30 hours a week and have time for my family and to exercise. I earn enough money to contribute to the family income and I love what I am doing!

One of the reasons for knowing your Vision Statement is so that you can check in with yourself and determine if what you are doing is getting you closer to achieving your goals. You know what business to say "yes" to, and what to say "no thanks" to.

The following is one definition of a mission statement from Wikipedia:

A mission statement is a brief statement of the company's core purpose and values. Companies

EXERCISE 2
DETERMINING YOUR VISION

Write your responses to the following questions — just let the thoughts flow easily from pen to paper.

Do this exercise with this thought in your mind: "I have my own home staging business."

1. **Why did I want to start my own business?** (For example, to be independent, to work when I want, to be my own boss, to work with positive clients, or to allow my creative side to come out.)

   _____

   _____

2. **What do I love to do in my business?** (For example, move furniture, organize spaces, help clients achieve their goals, write articles, make a sale, or create beautiful spaces.)

   _____

   _____

3. **What will I have others do for me in time?** (For example, bookkeeping, website design, ghost writing, setting up appointments, or moving furniture.)

   _____

   _____

4. **When I am successful I will** _____ .
   (complete the sentence)
   (For example, buy myself a new watch, have my own home staging television show, refer new clients because I am too busy, or get up each day with a smile on my face.)

Create Your Vision Statement

My Company Vision

_____

_____

_____

_____

_____

sometimes use their mission statement as an advertising slogan, but the intention of a mission statement is to keep members and users aware of why the organization exists and what it hopes to accomplish.

Your mission statement will keep you focused on your core business and your reasons for being in business. Your mission statement might say something like this:

My company provides quality state-of-the-art home staging services to realtors and home sellers so that their property has broad-target buyer appeal. Our home staging services exceed client expectations and are delivered on time, and on budget. We stage — you sell!

Exercise 3 will help you determine your company's mission statement.

1.3 History and background

The history and background is the section of your business plan that sells *you*. Even if you are not planning on getting financial help this is a great section to complete so you have a better understanding of why you are entering into this business. This will show you that you know what you are doing and that you are capable of being a home staging entrepreneur.

Think of it somewhat like your résumé if you were applying for a job. What do you want someone to know about you that would make you an incredibly successful home staging entrepreneur?

This section would include but is not limited to information such as:

- **Previous work experience:** especially anything related to home staging or an industry-related area such as working in a paint store, home decor, furniture store, etc.

- **Education and training:** in home staging or an industry-related area such as interior decorating, professional organizing, etc.

- **Awards:** anything that would indicate you are a high achiever or have done something that was worthy of some kind of recognition.

- **Volunteer work:** industry related or something that shows good character traits.

- **Entrepreneurial skills:** create a list of skills that you believe will help you be successful in the home staging industry.

- **Summary of qualifications:** wrap it all up in a few sentences. Remember, this is the time to brag!

1.4 Operations and description of the business

Specific information is required in the operations and description of the business portion of a business plan. You will include the name of your business, location, and contact information. You will need to decide how you will operate your business (i.e., as a sole proprietor, partnership, or corporation: structures which are discussed in more detail in Chapter 4.)

Describe the services that you will be offering as a home stager. Chapter 10 describes a variety of services that you may be qualified to offer your clients. You need to give some thought to whether or not you want to have inventory (i.e., small or major inventory) or no inventory. If you decide to have major inventory, you will need to factor in the storage and moving costs. Even if you only have a small inventory, you may still need to rent a storage locker.

EXERCISE 3
DETERMINING YOUR COMPANY'S MISSION STATEMENT

Answer the following questions using the "green light thinking" technique:

1. **The purpose of my company is:**

   _____
   _____

2. **My primary clients are:**

   _____
   _____

3. **My responsibilities towards my clients are:**

   _____
   _____

4. **The important values that I bring to my clients are:**

   _____
   _____

Create Your Company's Mission Statement

My Company Mission Statement

_____
_____
_____
_____
_____

Another factor to write about is whether or not you will have employees. Chapter 13 discusses the pros and cons of hiring employees versus hiring contractors. Most home stagers begin with hiring home staging contractors since they do not yet know their workload.

1.5 Market research and sales plans

In the market research and sales plans you need to go into detail about what you discovered from your market research (e.g., who your target market is, how you will market to them, and why they are going to buy from you).

One of the first and most important pieces of research you need to have done is to know whether or not home staging is a viable business in your marketplace. One of the best ways to judge this is to find out who else is doing home staging and how successful they are. You may be able to uncover information directly from another home stager or you may have to do some digging by talking with realtors and other industry-related professionals. You can look at others' success to help determine whether your business will be a financial success or not.

Included in this section are the details describing your target market (e.g., what gender the majority of your market will be, what age range, what their income level is, where they hang out, and how you will find them). This is important information that will help you determine which marketing strategies are going to work best for you to attract your ideal target market clients. Your sales strategies go hand in hand with your marketing strategies. For example, if you live in an area where your target market is not going to find you through social media sites, you need to find out ways to be able to connect with that group to be able to sell to them.

Also to be considered here is your *unique selling proposition*: What is going to make you stand out from another home stager? Every home stager comes with a totally different background than another home stager. Think about something you have done in the past that would serve you well as a home stager. Or, perhaps you have something that only you can offer in your area. Put yourself into your clients' minds: Why will they choose you over someone else? Include this to support why your target market is going to choose your home staging business over another one.

Chapter 3 offers some good information on how to conduct your market research.

1.6 Financial plan

The financial plan is the main part of your business plan if you are looking for investors or lenders. These potential money lenders will be scrutinizing every detail in this section! They mainly want to know that you have a sound business plan and that this will be a good investment for them. They are going to look at the small details here so be very diligent in gathering this information.

Most home stagers are not experts in doing financial statements so you might want to engage the services of an accountant or a financial planner. You will need to provide financial information about your expected revenues and expected expenses. If you have already started up your business, you will have some information to work from. If you have not, you will have to do the best you can with the information you have gathered from a variety of sources.

Your financial plan will show your income statement (also known as your profit and loss statement), balance sheet, and your cash-flow statement. Again, if you are unsure how to do this hire a professional as it will be worth it if you are looking for lenders.

Chapter 9 includes information about start-up costs so review that chapter to assist you with writing this section of your business plan.

1.7 Forecasts and projections

The forecasts and projections section can be somewhat of a challenge if you are at the beginning stages of your business. You are assuming that you will have a viable business so now you need to make your financial projections for both short- and long-term goals of your company.

Use the information provided to you in Chapter 9 to help you determine your short-term goals for revenues and expenses. You may not be venturing into this full time to begin with so if you have other income, you need to factor this into your business plan. Determine how much money you need to make and explain how you will make it; for example, through X number of staging clients I will make X number of dollars. Determine what you will be spending while you are growing your business.

Your business plan needs to contain some longer-term goals of five years and more. While this can be tricky due to economic conditions that you cannot control, your business plan still needs to have some evidence of being sustainable in the long term.

Complete Exercise 4 with as much of this information as you can to help you form your business plan.

2. Revisiting Your Business Plan

In the beginning it is best to check your business plan every six months just to make sure you are on track with your goals and your plans for achieving them.

Once you have been in business for a few years it is much easier to see where your money is coming from and what you are spending it on. If needed, you make your corrections when you see that something is not working and increase something that is working for your business. Even the best planners sometimes have to make adjustments and change their business model. There is nothing wrong with making changes that make your business more profitable for you.

EXERCISE 4
BUSINESS PLAN

1. Title page: Your company name, location, and contact information

   _____

   _____

   _____

2. Your company vision and mission statements

   _____

   _____

   _____

3. Determine if you are operating as a —

   [   ] Sole Proprietorship

   [   ] Partnership

   [   ] Corporation

4. Your background and/or other key personnel involved. List your accomplishments in other business areas to show your transferable skills to your new business. If you are hiring employees (e.g., bookkeepers, assistant), describe their roles in the business.

   _____

   _____

   _____

   _____

   _____

   _____

   _____

   _____

   _____

5. Your goals for your business

   Weekly:

   _____

   _____

Monthly:

_____

_____

First Year:

_____

_____

Second Year:

_____

_____

Third Year:

_____

_____

6. Business description: Describe the services you will provide or the products you will sell.

_____

_____

7. Competitor information: List your competitors and the services they provide. What makes your business different from them? What is your niche market to make you unique from your competitors?

_____

_____

8. Marketing plans: Describe your target market (e.g., demographics, age, income level, professions). Where will you find your clients? How will you market to them?

_____

_____

9. Start-up costs (e.g., office costs, supplies, tools, marketing materials) and where you will get the finances to start your business.

_____

_____

10. Financial goals: Determine monthly targeted revenues, monthly targeted expenses, profit, and loss.

_____

_____

3
Market Research

Before you start a new business it is paramount to your success that you do market research. As a home stager you need to know if what you are venturing into is needed in your area. In other words, do you know if people will buy your home staging services? If so, who are they and where will you find them? It is actually good news if you have competitors in your area because it lets you know that people know what home staging is, and you can find out what your competitive advantage is going to be based on who is doing what, and where.

1. Researching the Competition

One of the benefits of being in the home staging industry is that home stagers should have public websites that provide you with a lot of valuable information about their businesses! The following are several ways you can find out what other home stagers are doing in your area:

- Check out websites of home stagers, home staging courses, and related associations.

- Do Internet searches with key words such as "home staging," "home stagers," "home decorating," and "staging services." Add your location in your key word search to find out what your local competitors are doing. It is a good idea to know what other stagers are doing in other parts of the country, and other countries, but you will want to know who the competition is in your area specifically.

- Take a look at your local and regional newspapers. Are any stagers running ads? Are there articles written on home staging? Do you see some advertorials offering home staging services?

- Attend trade shows because they are a terrific resource to see who is doing what and get firsthand information by checking out your competition in person.

- ↳ Read magazines that are running articles and advertisements about home staging.

- ↳ Tune in to real estate radio talk shows to find out who is promoting home stagers.

- ↳ Watch local and national television shows that interview home stagers. There are many home staging shows on television now, so you may be able to pick up tips for your business.

- ↳ Look for real estate agent booths set up at shopping malls. Check out their photos and ask if they use a home stager and, if so, find out who they use.

- ↳ Join a networking group where small business people go to connect. Start attending some groups as a guest and find out who, if any, are in the home staging business.

- ↳ Check out real estate agents' websites to see if they have named a home staging company or person that they use to get their clients' homes ready for selling.

- ↳ Contact home stagers that are willing to help new home stagers. If asked, they may be willing to talk with you by phone or in person. This is worth trying as you may end up working together or referring each other at a future time.

In Exercise 5 you are going to do some research. This is a great exercise to help you make some comparisons with other home stagers and give some thought to what is going to make your business different.

Once you have gathered your data in Exercise 5 take some more time to think about how you will be different from these existing home staging businesses. Complete Exercise 6 to figure out your competitive advantage.

1.1 Your competitors as collaborators

Home staging is one of the few industries in which a competitor can actually become a collaborator. Most home staging businesses are owner operated and when extra help is needed for a job, work is contracted out to someone with the appropriate skill set. You may find yourself with a job that requires other home stagers' help, and being friendly and aware of who you could work with will aid your success.

Many home stagers who belong to associations work together cooperatively and give home staging a good name for everyone involved.

2. Researching Your Target Markets

Any successful business, large or small, begins by finding out who it could sell its products or services to. The home staging business has three primary targets:

- ↳ Home sellers

- ↳ Real estate agents

- ↳ Builders

Your secondary targets are people who can refer you to their clients:

- ↳ Strategic alliances (e.g., industry-related businesses)

- ↳ Anyone who knows someone selling their home

EXERCISE 5
COMPARISON CHART FOR EXISTING HOME STAGING BUSINESSES

Company Name/Years in Business	Owner Credentials	Home Staging Services	Prices	Target Market	What Makes Them Different?

Strategic alliances will be discussed in detail in Chapter 14 as secondary sources. Other sources will be discussed in Chapter 7, section **2**.

2.1 Home sellers

According to the United States' and Canadian censuses from 2006 to 2009, the average number of homeowners in North America was 67 percent. While this percentage may go up and down depending on economic upturn or downturn, it indicates that there are a high percentage of people who own their homes. At some point in time they will be selling their homes to either upsize or downsize, or as an investment.

2.1a Private home sales — for sale by owner (FSBO)

Some home sellers will sell their homes themselves. These people will use websites and other marketing strategies to help them sell their homes. It has recently been reported by the National Association of Realtors (NAR)

that 90 percent of home buyers are using the Internet to search listings.

Just because an owner is selling privately does not mean that the person won't use your home staging services. It's worthwhile to research private seller sites on the Internet that apply to your area. By looking at the photos on the website you can tell if the home has been staged or not. If not, phone and offer your services.

2.1b Identifying private and public home sellers

You might think that only affluent people with disposable income and large homes would use home stagers. However, this is not the case. Many one-bedroom condo owners will spend money on hiring a home stager because they know staging works. Other people with large, luxurious homes don't necessarily think their homes need to be staged. It really is a wide-open market when it comes to who uses home

EXERCISE 6
WHAT IS YOUR COMPETITIVE ADVANTAGE?

1. What do you like about the competitor's business?

    _____

    _____

    _____

    _____

    _____

2. What don't you like about the competitor's business?

    _____

    _____

    _____

    _____

    _____

3. What could you incorporate into your business without directly copying the other home staging business?

    _____

    _____

    _____

    _____

    _____

4. What would you do differently or better?

    _____

    _____

    _____

    _____

    _____

stagers and who does not. In some US states, sellers would not dream of selling their homes without having it staged first!

You can easily spot homes that are for sale by the "For Sale" sign they have on their lawns, or in the case of condominiums and apartments, signs in front of the building. From there you can either go to an open house if they are having one, or view the inside of the home via the Internet posting. You may also know people who are selling their homes that you can offer your services to. How you approach them to sell and market your services is discussed in detail in Chapter 7.

2.1c Characteristics of great home sellers as clients

It might not seem sensible to say that you do not want every client with a pulse and a check book; however, once you start growing your business and attracting new clients you can determine the type of clients with which you work best. Take a look at Exercise 7 and decide what type of clients you want to do business with.

Hopefully you have answered a resounding "Yes" to all of the characteristics that you are willing to accept when you work with your clients! Feel free to add other characteristics that are important to you to your list.

EXERCISE 7
WHAT TYPE OF CLIENTS DO YOU WANT TO WORK WITH?

	Client Characteristic	Yes	No
1.	Respects my professional recommendations.		
2.	Is open to looking at how he or she needs the home to look for selling and not for living.		
3.	Willing to do his or her homework before I arrive to do the hands-on home staging.		
4.	Works cooperatively with me to get the home ready for selling on time and on budget.		
5.	Happily pays me for my work in full, on time with a smile.		
6.	If other tradespeople are involved, the client will advise me if there are any holdups associated with the work I need to do.		
7.	Has a positive attitude and is a pleasure to work with.		

2.2 Realtors

The National Association of Realtors (NAR) in the United States boasts approximately 1.1 million members as of January 2010. In February 2010, the Canadian Real Estate Association (CREA) claims that there are more than 96,000 realtors across Canada. Regardless of where you live it would seem that there are sufficient numbers of realtors to contact about your home staging business. It would make good business sense to find out from your local real estate offices just how many realtors there are in your area. If you have a chapter of a national real estate association in your area, you should sign up for the association's e-newsletter as it will keep you apprised of your local market.

You might think that every realtor would have a relationship with a home stager but interestingly enough, this is not the case. Home staging is still breaking ground in many areas of the world. The more savvy real estate agents use home stagers as their best marketing tool. Some realtors think they know what makes a home look good and would not call on a home stager. Other realtors are having moderate success selling homes and are not convinced that home stagers are necessary in their market. It is up to you to convince a realtor that you are a good investment of his or her time, money, and energy.

The good news is that realtors are easy to find! The following are some of the places you are most likely to find them:

- Weekly real estate papers or flyers
- Company websites, which list every realtor with a link to each realtor's site
- Local offices — every office will have a list of all of its realtors signed up with each office, so you can easily obtain this list
- Advertising on buses and benches
- Open house signs — realtors names are posted on their signs
- Coffee shops — realtors often leave their cards on display for anyone to take
- Local radio or television shows — many areas have dedicated radio and television programs to real estate news
- Networking groups — most realtors belong to at least one networking group in their area; more and more business networking groups are popping up all over the world as small businesses grow and use the networking venue as a place to connect with other people
- Friends and family members are likely to recommend realtors they know or have worked with

While you are starting out, and even once you have established your business, it is a good idea to make sure you are building great working relationships with the realtors that you work with.

Now is a good time to make another list of all the great characteristics you want your realtors to have. It may take a few trial and error attempts to find the best match for yourself. You want to attract a relationship that is mutually beneficial and you know you can rely on to be behind you 100 percent. The realtor should feel the same way about you.

It is a good idea to take a look at your list once in a while to see if you are working with the type of home seller and/or realtor that compliments your work and gives referrals to your home staging business.

2.3 Home builders

Depending on where you live you may be fortunate to have new homes being built that require show homes to be staged for potential buyers.

Private home builders may build one home a year or multiple homes throughout the year. Many of the more savvy builders will require home staging services. Typically, with a smaller builder, they will rent the inventory from you on a monthly basis.

Public home builders who do large development projects typically stage one of the show homes. Depending on how many buildings they have on the go, and the timing of completion, builders will require home stagers to purchase furnishings to stage the show home so that they can use these furnishings in other buildings when needed. This is more cost-effective for them rather than renting inventory. (See Chapter 10 for more information on rental inventory.)

4
Legal Business Requirements

Every state, province, and country varies somewhat in the processes that you must go through to ensure you have followed all of the required procedures to legally set up your business. It is important to ensure you know what the legal requirements are in your area and that you have followed them.

In the United States, a good government resource is Business.gov. This is the US government's official website for small businesses. Business.gov provides access to federal, state, and local information that helps business owners successfully start and operate while staying compliant with laws and regulations.

In Canada, one of the best government resources to find information about setting up your business name, registering, and determining which taxes you are obligated to pay is CanadaBusiness.ca.

1. Business Name

Deciding on your business name can be a very thrilling event since it implies you are really going to start your home staging business! Before you start the process, I have a few words of advice for you:

- Have several name choices (minimum three) as you may not get your first choice (i.e., someone else may have already registered it as a business name or domain name).

- Once you have decided on your name, conduct an Internet search to make sure no one else has the URL you want. A URL is also called a domain name. In Canada, it is important to have both .ca and .com domains since most people will use .com first. Your webmaster can set it up so both domains go to one site.

⤙ Always have the *same* business name as your website name.

Picking a business name is a very big decision for you since this name and everything about it is going to represent you and your company. You can also use your own name if you choose. In Chapter 6 you will learn more about branding your business and your name choice is going to be key to identifying your brand attributes. Try Exercise 8 and give yourself lots of time to be a bit playful with the names as well.

Now is a good time to get some objective feedback. Many large corporations pay handsomely for focus group input, but for you I recommend a more cost-effective approach! Run your list by different people whom you think have good business judgment (not necessarily your best friends). You might want to ask some realtor friends and/or industry-related contacts what they think of your choices. The final decision is yours; however, getting feedback from different groups is a good thing throughout your decision-making times.

1.1 Deciding on a tagline or slogan for your business

Sometimes when you do the exercise of selecting your name, you come up with words that don't necessarily become part of your name, but still resonate with you. Think about incorporating some of these words or feelings into your tagline. Taglines or slogans communicate the *value proposition of an idea*. You might be familiar with ones such as American Express' "Don't leave home without it," or Nike's "Just Do It!" or Coca-Cola's "The pause that refreshes."

A tagline or slogan can be changed over time but it is never recommended that you keep changing your business name.

Here are two taglines that I have used over the years for my home staging business:

⤙ Remember … the way you LIVE in your HOME, is not the way you SELL your HOUSE

⤙ Transforming LIVES, by Transforming HOMES!

1.2 Business name approval

Once you have finally decided on your company's business name, you need to find out whether or not that name is available for you to register as your own. Most areas in North America have websites where you can do your search online to find out if the name you want is available. You can do this search by state, province, or federally if you want to get name approval for the entire country database. You can also complete the appropriate forms and mail them in, but of course this takes longer and most people want to secure the name they decided on right away! You will pay a small fee to submit your business name approval form.

Remember that once you have decided on your business name, do an Internet search with a website that does searches for domain names such as GoDaddy.com or Netfirms.com to see if the name you want is available. As mentioned earlier, if you are in Canada I recommend that you get both .ca and .com domain names. If you are in another country, I recommend getting one for your country and a .com one if you want worldwide recognition.

When you contact your government name-approval registry the staff will indicate how many names you can submit. In some countries they take three name submissions. They will notify you which business name is available. If the first name on your list is available, they will not search their database any further. If all of the names you have submitted are taken (i.e., already approved for someone else),

EXERCISE 8
CHOOSING YOUR COMPANY NAME

Let's do some "green light thinking" in which you write down whatever comes into your mind first with no censoring whatsoever:

1. List as many words as you can that describe your personality:

    _____

    _____

    _____

2. Write down three of your favorite colors and beside each one, write any words that you feel about each color:

    _____

    _____

    _____

3. Write down as many business names as you can think of that you like. Beside each name write down why you like the name.

    _____

    _____

    _____

4. Think about business logos that you like. What is something unique about you that could be translated into a logo?

    _____

    _____

    _____

5. Take a look at your mission statement again. Your target market needs to feel a connection with your company name. What words in your mission statement will appeal to your target market?

    _____

    _____

    _____

Once the ideas have stopped flowing — stop! You can come back to this exercise again and again until you have a name that sounds and feels good to you. Review your list and circle or highlight words, colors, and phrases that appeal to you. Narrow down the list until you have six to ten names that you like. If you only have three names, that might be all you need. The key is that the names resonate with you and you feel good about your choices. Write down your choices for your company name:

1. _____
2. _____
3. _____
4. _____
5. _____
6. _____
7. _____
8. _____
9. _____
10. _____

you will have to resubmit new options and pay another fee to go through the process again.

If a name is available, you will then have a predetermined number of days to accept the business name. During this grace period no one else can get the same business name approved. However, once this time lapses and you have not registered your company name, then someone else can legally take the name you submitted.

1.3 Business name registration

The next step in the process is registering the business name that has been approved. You will need to contact the business registration government agency in your area. You will pay another small fee to register your business name. This can also be done online or in person at a government-agency registry office in your area. Once your business name is registered you will be given a business number. This business number will stay with you for the life of your company.

2. Business Number

Your business number will be required for any and all government reporting purposes applicable to your business. Each state or province and country will have business taxes that you will need to start paying as soon as you begin accepting payment for your home staging services.

In the United States, for tax purposes you will be given your Tax Identification Number (TIN), and Employer Identification Number (EIN) assigned by the Internal Revenue Service (IRS) to business entities operating in the United States for the purposes of identification.

In Canada, you will apply through the Canada Revenue Agency for a Business Number (BN). If you want to open another company, your primary business name and number will be still used but you will fill out a form saying you are "Doing Business As" and the government agency will give you another number added on to your original business number.

3. Choosing Your Company Structure

Another question you will be asked on your business name approval form is about the structure you will use in your business. As a home stager you can choose to do business as a sole proprietor, partnership, or corporation.

You can change your structure at any time in the life of your business although you will always have the same business number. Future companies will be considered "Doing Business As" companies under your original business name and number.

There are many websites and resources that can help you find out more about the structure that is best for your new company.

3.1 Sole proprietorship

The sole proprietorship is the oldest, most common, and simplest form of business organization. A sole proprietorship is a business entity owned and managed by one person. The sole proprietorship can be organized very informally; it is not subject to much federal, state, or provincial regulation and is relatively simple to manage and control.

A key characteristic of a sole proprietorship is that the owner is inseparable from the business. Because they are the same entity, the owner of a sole proprietorship has complete control over the business and its operations, and is financially and legally responsible for all debts and legal actions against the business. Taxes on a sole proprietorship are determined at the personal income tax rate of the owner. In other words, a sole proprietorship does not pay taxes separately from the owner.

A sole proprietorship is a good business organization for an individual starting a business that will remain small, does not have great exposure to liability, and does not justify the expenses of incorporating and ongoing corporate formalities. The majority of home staging businesses start as sole proprietorships. You can change your structure at any time by reapplying to the appropriate government agency and paying the required fees.

In some areas, if you decide to set up your business structure as a sole proprietorship using your own name, without adding any other words, then business name registration may not be necessary.

As a sole proprietor home stager you will find that *you* are your business! This is why branding is so important.

3.2 Partnership

In a legal partnership, two or more people or companies combine their talents and resources to conduct the business. Many partnerships require a certain amount of capital to be invested by each partner. In a *general* partnership all partners are personally liable for all obligations of the company. A *limited* partnership is liable only up to the amount of equity invested.

The best scenario if you do decide to partner with another home stager is to find someone who has strengths that complement your weaker areas. For example, if you are not a good salesperson, look for a partner who has this skill set; you may be very good at installations or hands-on staging while your partner may be better suited to the business aspects. Each partner's responsibilities need to be clearly defined, preferably in a partnership agreement, which may not reflect the amount of money each partner invested in the beginning.

While many home stagers start out thinking that having a partner is a great idea, it has been my experience that most partnerships dissolve over time unless they are a true partnership with a formal written agreement between all partners. If you want to have a legal partnership, it is recommended that you hire legal counsel and meet with an accountant before you move forward. An accountant will inform you of the appropriate investments that all partners need to make, discuss tax scenarios and when the appropriate time is for you to enter into a partnership.

The reason you want to have a legal partnership agreement is to ensure that all parties and the company assets will be fairly treated should you or your partner want to dissolve the partnership. The legal partnership agreement is about the "What happens if... ?" scenarios that could occur in your business arrangement.

Most home stagers find other stagers to work with and call it a partnership, but actually they are just working together with no written agreement binding them to each other's business liabilities. In reality, they are doing business as contractors, which is the more common arrangement amongst home stagers. (Learn more about building strategic alliances in Chapter 14.)

A partnership can be dissolved at any time but it is recommended that you seek professional advice *before* entering into any partnership. If it is a two-person partnership, and one person dies or declares bankruptcy, then the partnership is normally dissolved; however, this scenario should be covered in your partnership agreement.

If you would like to learn more about partnership agreements, Self-Counsel Press publishes *Partnership Agreement* in Canada, or *The Small-Business Contracts Handbook* in the US.

3.3 Incorporation

When you incorporate your company you are creating a new legal entity. There are many reasons that home stagers might incorporate their businesses.

The following are some reasons for considering incorporating:

- Personal liability protection (most often, this is the reason home stagers incorporate)

- Substantial tax advantages and tax shelters (current and future if you want to sell your home staging business)

- A high degree of flexibility in personal financial planning

- Greater control in transferring ownership

- Easier to bring in outside investors and partners, which may be needed to fund the start-up of your business

- An incorporated company can survive an owner or shareholder's death (i.e., the company may last indefinitely)

I recommend you talk with both a lawyer and an accountant asking for their input based on your personal assets and your projected earnings. If you are considering incorporating, you should consult a lawyer.

4. Business License

Almost every business is required to have a business license if they want to conduct their business legally. Just about all businesses need a city, township, or county business license. Most home stagers operate their businesses out of their homes, but they may still require a business license that is renewable on a yearly basis. There may also be other local, county, state or provincial, and federal licensing requirements. The fees associated with purchasing the license vary from country to country and it is another cost of doing business that is, of course, tax deductible.

Before you apply for a business license there are a few licensing requirements you might want to be aware of, including:

- ✔ If you have a home office and you are planning on remodeling it, you may be required to get a permit to do so.

- ✔ If you have a home office in an apartment or condo building, you may require written permission from the strata council indicating you are allowed to operate your business in your suite.

- ✔ As a home stager you may decide to rent or lease a storefront location if you have inventory that you offer to the general public or other stagers as one of your business lines.

- ✔ Check to see if you need a zoning compliance permit before you open your business. Make sure the space you own or lease is properly zoned for your staging business.

When you do apply for a business license you will need to provide some or all of the following:

- ✔ Government identification (e.g., driver's license, passport)

- ✔ Proof of address (a driver's license will do)

- ✔ If you are a limited liability company or a corporation, then you need your certificate for proof

If you live in a strata building, you will be required to provide the document that indicates you can have approval to operate a business out of your home.

5. Business Taxes

We have all heard the famous quote by Benjamin Franklin, "In this world nothing can be said to be certain except death and taxes." I would prefer that you focus on being alive and excited about starting your new home staging business and consider paying taxes as just another part of doing business! As a home staging business owner you may be required to pay some or all of these taxes: municipal, state or provincial, and federal taxes.

5.1 Federal sales taxes

In the United States, sales taxes are imposed by state and local administrations, of which there are more than 40,000. Merchants (shops and other sellers) charge the customer a combined rate which bundles together the state tax with the tax of the locality in which they sell. Depending on the locality, the merchant then either pays the tax to the state administration, which unbundles it and remits the locality's share, or pays the state and the local administration their shares separately.

A seller has to charge sales tax if it has nexus where it is located. Nexus, or substantial physical presence, is established if a business maintains a temporary or permanent presence of people (i.e., employees, service people, or independent sales/service agents) or property (i.e., inventory, offices, warehouses) in a given locality. There is no over-arching definition of nexus, so each taxing locality may define it differently — and many do, leading to endless problems for businesses which have operations in multiple states.

Not all products are subject to sales tax, and states differ in the exemptions they offer. The rates of sales tax may also vary within a state for different types of business. All but five states impose a general sales tax at the state level (Alaska, Delaware, Montana, New Hampshire, and Oregon are the exceptions), but even in these five states some localities impose their own sales taxes, and some of the five impose sales taxes on particular products or services. It is best to check with your state and know exactly what taxes you have to pay and when.

In Canada, the federal sales tax is the goods and services tax (GST). Just to complicate matters, in July 2010, the provincial and federal taxes changed across the country so that some provinces were paying a new tax called a harmonized sales tax (HST) which included their provincial sales tax (PST) and the GST. The percentages of taxes vary throughout the country as well. In Canada, you need to contact the Canada Revenue Agency (CRA) and apply for your GST or HST number. You are required to commence paying these taxes once your sales reach $30,000 in four consecutive quarters or in one calendar year. All of the information you will need to know can be found on the CRA's website.

In order to apply for the GST or HST number you will then be required to have your Business Number. You can do this online as well. If you have other businesses under the "Doing Business As" name, your GST or HST number will stay the same for them as well.

I recommend that you continue to be apprised of regulations that you need to comply with at all times.

5.2 State and provincial sales taxes

Aside from federal taxes, the United States and Canada require that as the owner of a home staging business you must also apply to obtain your state sales tax number or provincial sales tax number (PST), if this is applicable. Interestingly enough, in Canada, if you are renting inventory to your client, you must also charge PST and then file your taxes accordingly. If you happen to be one of the provinces that is now paying HST, the PST is part of that tax now.

Depending on how quickly you grow your business you will most likely begin by filing your tax reports on an annual basis. However, as you grow your business you may be required to file quarterly. The amount you will be paying in future years is typically based on the previous year's sales.

You should research your state or province's rules on government sales tax regulations as each area is different. You may also want to talk to a business lawyer or an accountant for more information on sales taxes.

5.3 Income tax

Sorry, but there is no way of getting around income tax! Depending on the structure of your business you will need to file your income tax on an annual basis. If you are good with bookkeeping and accounting, you may decide to file yourself. However, if you are not good with numbers or tax forms, I highly recommend you have a professional do your taxes for you. If you have an incorporated business, you must have an accountant file your taxes for you.

5
Insurance

Before you start your home staging business I recommend that you determine what insurance you will need. Some of your insurance is a legal requirement. For example, if you have employees, you must pay Workers' Compensation. In some general commercial liability insurance policies it will state that anyone whom you contract with must have their own insurance. If not, your insurance may be null and void. However, it makes sense that you have insurance so you have peace of mind and are prepared if something unforeseen happens.

When you do your research, check out at least three different insurance companies and make sure you are comparing "apples to apples" when you look at the policies.

1. Home Insurance

Most home stagers have a home office. Your existing home insurance policy may allow you to have a "rider" on your policy. A rider

provides additional coverage for something specifically not covered with a primary policy. The rider is added to the primary policy and the policy holder pays an extra amount to cover the rider. Not every insurance company will allow a rider so you need to conduct some due diligence here.

You want your homeowner's insurance to cover the following business items:

- ⚶ Computer or laptop
- ⚶ Cell phone or BlackBerry/iPhone
- ⚶ Printer and/or fax machine
- ⚶ Office furniture
- ⚶ Other computer-related equipment such as microphones, headsets, and webcams
- ⚶ Camera

It is equally important for you to find out if the home sellers have homeowner's insurance as well. Rental furnishings can be damaged, stolen, or broken, especially if someone is still living in the home. Sellers' homeowners' insurance will cover your goods or another company's rentals.

The best way to ensure that homeowners are taking responsibility for your rental furnishings in their homes is to have them sign your contract stating that they have their own insurance and are responsible for the goods. Even if they do not have insurance they are still responsible and your signed agreement states that clearly.

Some home stagers have decided to charge a refundable damage deposit of several hundred dollars which the homeowner gets back if everything is returned in the same condition as it was rented.

Something you may not know is that if the home seller has renters and you are providing rentals in that rental suite, the renters should also have their own insurance. Ask your insurance agent to find out more about this.

The cost of home insurance depends on where you are located. As an example, the cost for insurance on business contents kept at an office or a home office may be $0.50 per $100 of insurance. So, if you had $10,000 of contents, the cost is $50. For mobile contents such as laptops and BlackBerrys the cost might be $4 per $1,000, so that $5,000 worth of mobile contents would cost $20. Deductibles in this example would be $1,000.

2. Business Insurance: Commercial Liability

Commercial liability insurance protects your business and you against lawsuits from other parties (third parties). Two things come into play before coverage is activated:

1. There must be bodily injury or property damage to third parties.

2. The injury or damage must have resulted from your negligence — negligence as defined by law (i.e., how a court interprets it). Sometimes it is obvious that you are negligent, but other times not so much. If it's not clear you are negligent, then your liability policy will most likely pay for lawyers to fight your case. Note that US courts' awards for negligence are much higher than those in Canadian courts.

An important component to running your home staging business is to have adequate business insurance coverage. In the beginning it will take time to find an insurance company that gives you good coverage. I recommend that you get three quotes from three different insurance brokers.

Years ago when home staging was not a well-known profession, stagers were considered either interior decorators or interior designers. In some places this is still the case. When talking to your insurance broker make sure you clearly define the type of work you will be doing.

A word of caution here: If you have your own inventory, and you are physically moving furniture on and off a truck, your insurance premiums will be much higher since the insurance company sees this activity as higher risk than doing consultations and moving furniture inside a home from room to room.

Please note that commercial insurance prices can vary day to day. If you were given a price for insurance today, there is no guarantee that the same price will be available tomorrow. Generally, insurance companies target certain types of businesses they are interested in insuring. At any given point in time, this can change. Often if a type of business they have targeted is losing money for them, they will either increase the cost or refuse to insure the business. Fortunately for home stagers, this business is considered relatively stable.

The cost of your commercial insurance depends on where you live and which insurance agent you deal with. It will also depend on your projected earnings. Commercial insurance is generally reviewed on an annual basis and, if there are no claims, it may be slightly increased each year since you will be making more money as you grow your business. As an example, for $1,000,000 liability limit with gross revenues of $50,000 or less, prices vary from $500 to $1,000 depending on the insurance company and your location; $2,000,000 would be from $650 to $1,000. The standard deductible in the event of a claim is $1,000 so most home stagers pay out-of-pocket for damages less than $1,000.

3. Cost of Your Inventory Coverage

When doing research in respect to inventory at vacant premises and at storage lockers, insurance companies vary greatly in their coverage. Some may agree to provide coverage, while others won't, and the costs for doing so vary greatly. However, if you do your research, you will find an insurance company that will give you coverage for the inventory in your storage locker. You will need to check with your insurance agent, but as an example, in one area the cost is about $0.50 per $100 of inventory.

For vacant premises your costs would be much higher. In one area it is about $2 per $100 of inventory. Contents insured on vacant or unoccupied properties are usually subject to very restrictive coverage. Theft and vandalism are usually *excluded* when premises are unoccupied. The best advice I can give you is to investigate

the cost and the kind of coverage that can be obtained whether it is broad coverage or restrictive.

Be aware of what your policy indicates about the *length of time* of your rental inventory coverage. If a home is vacant and does not sell right away, you need to be crystal clear about how long the inventory is covered for, and for how much.

4. Rental Furnishing Company's Coverage

If you have your home seller rent directly from a rental inventory company, the insurance coverage is between those two parties. While some home stagers like to be able to mark up inventory, if you do that, you may become responsible for the rentals. If the rentals are not returned in their original condition (e.g., not damaged, soiled, or broken), you will be responsible for the charges.

5. Workers' Compensation

In both the United States and Canada you are not legally required to have Workers' Compensation insurance unless you have employees. Most home stagers hire other stagers as contractors; you are not responsible for Workers' Compensation coverage for the contractors.

While this is optional insurance coverage, you may decide it is a good thing for you to have should you get injured on the job. The cost of your Workers' Compensation will be based on the category you are in. The amount you will receive is a predetermined rate until you prove you have higher gross monthly earnings than what they use for the average claim.

In the United States you can go to Business.gov and search with the words "Workers' Compensation"; the search will direct you to a link which has direct links for every state.

In Canada you can apply for Workers' Compensation. Each province has a different plan that protects you against wage loss, and may provide medical and rehabilitation services if you are injured while on the job or if you contract a disease as a result of your work. The plan includes people who are self-employed, as well as partners, proprietors, and proprietor spouses in a non-limited company. For more information go to the website of the Association of Workers' Compensation Boards of Canada (AWCBC.org).

6. Critical Injury or Disability

Critical injury or disability insurance is another optional insurance coverage that you can have. It can be up to $100 per month and varies from state to state and province to province. Again,

many self-employed home stagers will get this coverage to gain peace of mind.

If you indicate you are loading and unloading furniture from a truck, your insurance will be considerably higher than if you are providing consultation services and only moving some furniture within a home.

7. Vehicle Insurance

As a professional home stager, it is highly recommended that you have good business-use vehicle insurance coverage for yourself and your vehicle. You may find yourself providing shopping services for your clients and using your vehicle to do this. You may also have one of your contractors as a passenger in your car. Make sure you have coverage for other parties that may be in your vehicle.

6
Branding Your Business

Next to actually doing the home staging work, one of the most fun and creative things you will do for your business is to brand it.

Many large corporations spend huge amounts of money on brand recognition. You are aware of brand names such as Coca-Cola, Pepsi, McDonald's, Disney, Nike, Apple, and Microsoft. Some companies have been exceptional at their branding; for example, if I were to say just the name of a person such as "Oprah," you immediately know who I am talking about and associate many qualities and characteristics with this brand.

Wikipedia offers us this definition:

Brand is the image of the product in the market. Some people distinguish the psychological aspect of a brand from the experiential aspect. The experiential aspect consists of the sum of all points of contact with the brand and is known as the brand experience. The psychological aspect, sometimes referred to as the brand image, is a symbolic construct created within
the minds of people and consists of all the information and expectations associated with a product or service.

People engaged in branding seek to develop or align the expectations behind the brand experience, creating the impression that a brand associated with a product or service has certain qualities or characteristics that make it special or unique. A brand is therefore one of the most valuable elements in an advertising theme, as it demonstrates what the brand owner is able to offer in the marketplace.

In other words, your brand symbolizes your *identity*, your *promise*, and the *experience* you will deliver to your ideal client every single time.

1. Why Your Brand Is Important

If you are a solo entrepreneur, you are your brand! If you have many contractors or employees, they will represent your brand for you. The better your branding is the higher probability of your company being thought about first rather than another home stager's company.

Advertising does play a role in keeping your brand uppermost in your target market's mind and will be discussed in Chapter 7.

Once you have established your brand you need to remain consistent in your delivery of your *brand promise*. By offering consistent and quality service, home sellers and realtors will start to remember who you are through your brand, even if you are not personally dealing with them.

2. Establishing Your Brand Image

If you are just starting out, or revisiting your business brand, you need to take some time to really think about who and what your brand represents to you and to your customers. It's unlikely you will have millions of dollars like the big players to invest in determining your brand, but there is a lot you can do to have very cost-effective branding.

Exercise 9 will help you get started assessing some of the characteristics and traits you want associated with your brand.

3. Your Brand Image Will Change over Time

It makes sense that if you are creating your brand for the first time, you may want to make changes later as you gain experience and start working with your customers. You may decide that some personality traits or characteristics that you thought were important in the beginning become less so, and others emerge that become very important to you and your brand.

When you do make changes to your branding, you want to make sure you do not change what have become the most *memorable qualities* of your brand. Before you make updates, make sure you know how people are recognizing your brand and what they love about your

brand. As you grow your business you will also become more authentic and understand more about yourself. Keep what you know has worked for you and stay consistent with this and then add, change, delete, or update as you see necessary.

4. Trademarking Your Brand

A trademark can be a word, slogan, symbol, or something else that serves as a unique or distinct indicator of the goods and/or services you provide. One of the advantages of owning a trademark is that you may seek remedies such as an injunction or monetary damages against a person who has infringed on your trademark or who has depreciated the value of its goodwill.

If you really want to ensure that no one else takes your name or your tagline, I recommend that you get it trademarked. Trademarking offers you one type of intellectual property protection. However, your trademark will only be good in the country of registration. If something is already trademarked, you cannot use it unless you have been given permission by the trademark owner.

Trademarks can be done nationally or internationally. You can conduct your own trademark search or hire a trademark specialist to do this for you. There is a lengthy process that you must go through to register a trademark. While you are awaiting approval of your trademark you can use this symbol: ™. It may take several years before your application is finalized. When you receive your documents indicating the trademark has been registered and that it is now yours, you can display it with this symbol: ®.

In both Canada and the United States you can do your own trademark search and registration by going to the websites of the

EXERCISE 9
YOUR BRAND'S CHARACTERISTICS AND PERSONALITY TRAITS

Check off all of the characteristics and personality traits listed below that you would like to be part of your brand:

[　] Professional	[　] Consistent
[　] Dynamic	[　] Edgy
[　] Dependable	[　] Mainstream
[　] Creative	[　] Reliable
[　] Stylish	[　] Respectful
[　] Energetic	[　] Trustworthy
[　] Authentic	[　] Service-oriented
[　] Friendly	[　] Quality provider
[　] Out-of-the-box thinking	[　] Organized
[　] Whimsical	[　] Flexible
[　] Can-do attitude	

In the book *The Boss of You: Everything a Woman Needs to Know to Start, Run, and Maintain Her Own Business*, written by entrepreneurs Lauren Bacon and Emira Mears, they equate your brand with your most memorable qualities. In their book they use the words "branding" and "personality" interchangeably and believe that personality is one of the major elements that drives customer loyalty. They suggest you imagine your business as a person (or an animate or inanimate object, if you prefer) and ask questions such as the following to dig deeper in understanding your brand:

Your Business Personality Quiz

1. If your business were to walk into the room, what would it be wearing?

   _____

   _____

   _____

2. What foods, drinks, movies, magazines, and travel destinations would appeal?

   _____

   _____

   _____

3. How would it interact with your customers?

_____

_____

_____

4. What colors, tastes, and smells come to mind when you think of your business?

_____

_____

_____

5. What kind of meal would reflect your business personality?

_____

_____

_____

United States Patent and Trademark Office or the Canadian Intellectual Property Office. It is advisable to consult a trademark lawyer or agent to oversee the trademark process and to provide advice on protecting and licensing your trademark.

Many people in the real estate industry have trademarked names, logos, and taglines. Many home staging schools offer trademarked or registered trademark designations. For my own business, PRES® Staging Resource Centre, I have a registered trademark that my member graduates use to indicate their professional designation as PRES® Professional Real Estate Stagers in the home staging industry. You will also notice other designations of home stagers such as CSP™, CRSS™, ASP®, HSE™, and IRIS® have all been trademarked and/or registered.

5. Key Marketing Pieces Needed to Secure Your Image

In today's marketplace all businesses need to have certain marketing materials to show that they are serious about doing business. While Chapter 7 is devoted to marketing strategies, and Chapter 8 is about marketing tools, keep in mind that, at the very least, while you are building your business you will need to have a professional looking business card and website.

You may decide to find or create your own logo and come up with your own tagline. From there you may decide to create your own business card and perhaps even your own website. Remember that if they are not top quality, this will be reflected in your brand. Are you promising a less-than-great experience with your business?

7
Marketing and Advertising Your Business

Marketing is one of the most critical components to your home staging business. Simply put, marketing is *informing* and *educating* your target market about the home staging services and products that you have to offer them. The reason you need to inform and educate people is simple: If people do not know about your services, they cannot buy your services.

Effective marketing allows you to —

  ✓ know who your target market is,

  ✓ attract your ideal clients, and

  ✓ successfully sell to this market.

If you are successfully selling to the right target market, who should also be your ideal clients, your business will grow. If you are not, your business will never get off the ground.

In Chapter 3 it was discussed in detail why it was necessary to research to find your target market. In this chapter you will find out how to promote your business to your target market using a variety of marketing strategies. Your goal is to come up with multiple strategies that will help you attract your target market to your business. Chapter 8 discusses the marketing tools you will need to implement your marketing strategies.

Whether you have an established business or not, there is never a time when you are not marketing your services if you want to see your business grow and thrive! Many new entrepreneurs make the mistake of thinking that once they have business cards and a website they can sit back and business will start to come in.

While business cards and websites are necessary and great tools to kick start your business, they are just two of the first marketing materials you will need to launch your business.

Once you are in your second or third year of business your business should start to grow through referrals and repeat clients. However, you will always market and sell your services according to your desired income goal. If you are doing this business part time and it meets your goals, you will spend less on marketing than someone who wants to do this full time. A higher dollar investment in excellent marketing strategies will be rewarded by a higher income. You do need to invest money to make money!

1. Marketing Strategies

One of the most important lessons I have learned since starting my home staging business is that my marketing strategies are constantly changing. What worked one year, or even one month, did not necessarily work the next year, or the next month. It is imperative that you recognize what is working in your market, and what is not. The most obvious way to know this is to look at your sales targets. Are you achieving them or not?

In Chapter 3 we identified *who* your target market would be in the area you plan on offering your home staging services. We identified your three primary target markets as the following:

- Home sellers (both private and public sales)
- Realtors (with buyers and sellers)
- Builders (with show homes)

We also identified your secondary target market to be your strategic alliances and people who know people who are selling their properties. So now that you know *who* you are marketing to, the following are the next questions to ask yourself:

- *Where* do I market my business?
- *How* do I market my business?
- *What* do I use to market my business?

Something to consider when you are determining your marketing strategies is this: It is *eight times* more expensive to look for new clients than to work with existing or past clients. If you are looking for new clients, they need to see you, your ad, or whatever method you are using to promote yourself 7 to 12 times in order for your business to stick in their minds!

2. Networking

Many people are uncomfortable with networking, yet it is one of the best methods for marketing yourself and your business. Networking is all about making connections with people you have not met before and developing relationships that can be mutually beneficial. Currently, the more tried-and-true form of networking is *business networking*. It still continues to prosper with new business models for private networking businesses expanding yearly. A newer method of making connections is through *social networking*, which is conducted through the Internet on a multitude of websites.

There are many existing not-for-profit networking groups and many growing for-profit networking groups. Since there are so many small businesses in the marketplace, networking is seen as critical for small-business owners such as home stagers, hence why networking aids growth in this industry.

It is important to find the right networking group that you feel the most comfortable with and get the most benefit from. Over time you will not renew some memberships, and you will also join others that are more representative of where you are at in your business model. As your confidence grows it makes sense that you will want to network with more powerful people as well.

2.1 How to network

When you attend networking events or when you meet someone casually and the person asks what you do, you want to be able to concisely and succinctly tell him or her what you do within 20 to 30 seconds. At some networking events you may have as long as one or two minutes to introduce yourself so you need to be prepared! This has been termed your "infomercial" or "elevator speech."

The term "elevator speech" is said to have originated from the idea that you have a captive audience in an elevator for only so much time until the elevator reaches its destination, to let someone know what you do. As North Americans we typically always ask people what they do when we first meet them regardless of the context. So as a new business owner it is important to get your elevator speech down pat.

Here are some tips on creating a great elevator speech that introduces you to a group:

- ↙ Make it interesting so people want to know more about you.

- ↙ Give good eye contact to a few people in the room or in your small group.

- ↙ Create a message that speaks to your target market.

- ↙ Let your audience know who your ideal clients are and what their problems are (you can focus on a different ideal client type each time and state a different problem if you are doing a weekly networking meeting so they understand you do more than just one thing).

- ↙ Include the *problem* your target market will have.

- ↙ Offer the target market the *solution*.

- ↙ Offer the target market the *results* they will obtain from your solution.

- ↙ Vary your talks and sometimes end with a question that invites them to ask you more.

- ↙ Inject some humor and use inflections when giving your speech.

- ↙ Come up with a *memorable tagline* to leave with them.

A key point to think about when creating your message is to think of what kind of *pain* your target market might be experiencing. That might seem an odd way to think about creating your elevator speech, but it is a well-known fact that once you find your target market's pain, you can offer a solution to relieve them of their pain. People in pain will listen because they want their pain to be gone! The situation may also develop where the people you are talking to do not need your pain remedy, but they may know of someone in their network who is in need of your services. This is also a great way for you to extend your *net* because someone else is now going to tell others about the fabulous home staging services that you have to offer!

This is an example of a good 20-second home stager's elevator speech:

"Hello my name is *(insert your name)*. My company is *(insert name of company)*. I take the stress out of preparing a house for selling. Most sellers are overwhelmed in the beginning. They struggle with questions such as what are the best paint colors? How much do I need to spend on home improvements? How do I do this? Do I need to do that? Where do I even start? In just a few short hours I can put together a report with their best return-on-investments, pick their paint colors, show them what to do, *and* I can stage their home in just one day. Sellers work with me to have less stress, more money, and energy left to move! Thank you, *(insert person's name)* with *(insert the person's company name)*."

If you only have a few seconds then try using just this short introduction:

"I take the stress out of preparing a house for selling. I can show you how to save thousands of dollars by telling you exactly where to spend your money for your best return-on-investment."

People should be interested in knowing how you do what you do, and since you have your longer elevator speech prepared, this will be easy for you!

The best way to be able to deliver your elevator speech with ease and confidence is by writing it down and memorizing it. If you have more than 30 seconds to introduce yourself, you can elaborate on what you do. It is a great idea to have testimonials on hand to read. They speak volumes about your work and how satisfied your clients are! If you are new to networking, there is nothing wrong with having your elevator speech written down and reading it. Over time you will be saying it automatically while you hand someone your business card. Recently I attended a networking event in which two of the members actually read their elevator speech off of their BlackBerrys!

Find a quiet time to create your elevator speech by using Exercise 10. Think about emotional pain as well as physical problems that the homeowners or the house may have before the house is ready for selling. After filling in your chart, write down your elevator speech.

2.2 Tips for positive networking

Over the years I have attended hundreds of networking functions. There are a few common mistakes that new networkers (and some who should know better) make. Here are a few tips to keep you on track so that you can avoid these mistakes and start networking on a positive note:

- Always have business cards with you because you can build your network anywhere, even standing in a grocery line, dentist's office, car wash, or hair salon.

- While networking is about you, it is important to really listen to what someone else is saying and see if you can refer the person to someone in your network who could assist him or her if you cannot.

- Ask questions that show you are interested in them (e.g., "How did you get started in your business, what do you find the most challenging, and can you describe your ideal client to me?").

- When it is your turn, have your elevator speech ready to go to introduce yourself with calmness and ease.

- Give good eye contact when speaking and listening; in other words, be present with them.

- Keep circulating at the event so that you do not monopolize any one person and so that one person is not monopolizing all of your time.

- Follow up with everyone that you met with an email, a phone call, or send them a card that is handpicked or electronic.

- Stay in touch with people that you felt a strong connection with because at some point in time you will probably do

EXERCISE 10
CREATING YOUR ELEVATOR SPEECH

Problems or Pain for Home Sellers	Require These Solutions	To Achieve These Results
E.g., Overwhelmed	Ease your stress	You get done what you need to
E.g., Old paint colors	New paint colors	Give your home a modern, refreshed look

business with them or with one of their referrals.

2.3 Benefits of business networking memberships

Once you decide on which networking groups you want to join, there are many benefits to becoming a member. Most importantly you will have more opportunities for greater exposure of your home staging business than non-members have and most events will cost you less than they do nonmembers. You may also have a mini-website in some member directories as well as be offered more "specials" than nonmembers, and reduced rates for workshops and other courses offered.

Many networking groups allow you the opportunity to participate on the board or become a volunteer so that you can meet and greet new members.

At larger networking functions, as a member, you will be able to set up a table display or a booth to promote your home staging business. Sometimes this is free, while other times you may pay a nominal fee. When you are giving your elevator speech it is a fantastic idea to let people know you have set up a table display and that you are giving away something for *free*. For example, in the beginning of your home staging business you might want to give away "One Day FREE Home Staging" or once you are more established, "One Hour FREE Home Staging Consultation." Make the gift appropriate to your market and the time that you have to do the freebies. You might also want to have people go to your website and sign up for your free ezine or report. This is a great strategy to get your database started!

The following sections discuss some networking groups you may want to research and see if they fit with your business.

2.3a Business networking

Business networking is a marketing strategy where people meet in person to promote their business by developing business relationships with others. Networking is a cost-effective way to generate new business leads and make connections with other like-minded people. Once you have met people at a networking event it is important to take the next step and follow up with those people you want to connect with more.

As a new home stager just starting, or even if you have been in business for a while, I recommend that you check out as many networking groups as you can. You will know which ones are going to be the right fit for you and your business by the response you get from other members, and ultimately the business you get.

Today's networking model implies that when we network we are there to give and help others make their businesses more successful as well. It is all about building relationships that are mutually beneficial so that you can grow a powerful network. *Work the Pond! Use the Power of Positive Networking to Leap Forward in Work and Life*, by Darcy Rezac (with Judy Thomson and Gayle Hallgren-Rezac), provides some great tips on networking to take the fear out of meeting people you do not know. The "Seven Secrets of Networking" take a light-hearted approach to networking and offer concrete examples of how you can network and become good at it.

Most networking groups will host a variety of functions such as breakfasts, lunches, dinners, special events, awards ceremonies, new member receptions, auctions, and golf tournaments. In order to get the most out of going to networking events that work for you, it is best that you join and become a member of the organization or business group.

Some networking groups such as Business Network International (BNI) will only allow one person per business sector to become a member. You may have to put yourself on a wait-list if there is already a home stager in the group.

When you are doing your research to determine the best groups to attend or join, complete Exercise 11 to help you make good business decisions. As your business grows you will become busier and have to determine which networking groups give you the best return-on-investment (ROI) of your time, money, and energy.

2.3b Women-only networking groups

When I first started marketing my business I tried a variety of marketing strategies. Networking was my most cost-effective marketing activity and my biggest return-on-investment! In my first year of business about 80 percent of my sales came directly from the people I had met while I was networking, and the majority of my connections were with women! This is an interesting statistic that I learned from a women-only networking event at which the guest speaker was Mary Charleson of Charleson Communications:

"Women buy or influence the purchases of 85 percent or more of what is sold. Yet a recent Canadian survey revealed that women's satisfaction level with many industries is well below 50 percent."

It stands to reason that if you target women and provide exceptional customer service, you have an excellent opportunity to grow your business with them.

There are many women-only networking events that you can find in your area by doing an Internet search. In the United States, eWomenNetwork has a national presence and is located in all major cities. They offer local

EXERCISE 11
NETWORKING COMPARISON CHART

Name of Group	Number of Members	Fees 1. Annual 2. Monthly 3. Events	Events	Member Benefits	Accepts Only One Type of Business Yes/No

and national events, workshops, e-newsletters, business tips, conferences, and a multitude of resources for starting and growing your business. There are several eWomenNetwork chapters across Canada as well.

In Canada a great resource for networking and learning how to network is the Women's Enterprise Centre. There are literally hundreds of networking groups you can join, such as a national women's network called Roaring Women, which offers a variety of events, resources, and local workshops for ongoing learning and networking opportunities.

2.3c Mixed-gender networking groups

Having shared my initial marketing successes with women, I learned it is equally important to go to mixed-gender networking events as well! Some of the more well-known networking groups for both men and women include:

ꙮ Chambers of Commerce (in your area)

ꙮ Boards of Trades (in your area)

ꙮ Private business networking groups such as Meetup, Business Network International (BNI), and SOHO (Canada)

Business and trade associations also offer networking, often on a monthly or annual convention-type basis.

2.3d Home staging networking groups

Whether you decide to take an online home staging course or an in-person course, once you have graduated, you will receive a designation indicating you are a professional home stager. Upon graduation you will be eligible to become a member of that home staging group which allows you to network with other home stagers of the same designation. Networking may take a variety of forms such as local meetings with guest speakers, industry-related field trips, teleconference calls, or webinars offered to all members.

In North America, as a professional home stager, you can join an international association called the Real Estate Staging Association (RESA). This is a member-governed trade association that offers education and business tools focusing on the needs of home stagers. RESA holds an annual international conference where members from all over North America can attend and network with one another, regardless of the designation they hold. They have guest speakers who are experts in their field talking on a variety of strategies to increase the success of your home staging business.

RESA also has local chapter meetings available to members in North America. These can be great networking opportunities and can provide ongoing learning.

2.4 Social media networking

As was mentioned earlier, marketing strategies have changed over the years and we can now add social media networking to our mix of strategies and tools.

According to social media guru Mhairi Petrovic, of Out-Smarts, most professional businesses need to use some form of social media tools such as wikis, blogs, and podcasts as well as social networking sites such as Facebook, LinkedIn, and YouTube, to name a few. These are all "online technologies," which allow you to share content and interact with others. Petrovic likes to make the analogy of connecting with your friends at a pub after work, only this time the connection is through the Internet.

Statistics that can be gathered from Internet searches indicate that while Facebook is currently the largest populated social media site, MySpace is also highly used as well as Twitter. Each site reaches a particular target market; for example, Facebook is popular for all ages and especially women 40 plus, while MySpace and Twitter are populated by younger bloggers and moms. There are hundreds of thousands of videos uploaded to YouTube and more than 180 million blogs. Seventy-seven percent of active Internet users use blogs, and the fastest growing demographic is people older than 35 with more women than men blogging. Now that's something to think about!

Petrovic sees some of the following benefits to using social media tools. You are able to:

- reach a wider targeted audience.
- grow your network and make new connections.
- maintain contact with existing networks.
- connect and learn from industry peers.
- establish your expertise and build brand awareness.
- promote your business.
- generate leads.
- drive traffic to your website or blog.

Since we know one of the keys to marketing is identifying your target market, for home stagers it is recommended that you take a look at Facebook and LinkedIn as these are two of the more appropriate sites on which to connect with your target market.

Active Rain is a fantastic real estate blog that warrants your investigation and one I encourage you to sign up for. The Active Rain community is comprised of close to 200,000 real estate and other industry-related professionals worldwide. You can increase your website rankings by being active on blogs such as these. You can comment on other people's blogs, join home staging groups, and write your own blog postings. This is a great tool to get yourself known as a home staging expert. You can subscribe to receive current topical information on a regular basis through a Really Simple Syndication (RSS) feed and respond to topics that interest you.

More social media tools will become available to businesses so it is important to always be up-to-date with new technologies when working on or updating your marketing plan.

3. Advertising

You need to determine what your advertising budget is before you decide on how you will advertise. Very often your first year of business can be one of your most expensive years, but without a doubt you need to make this investment. It is an investment of not only your money but your time and energy. You can get a lot of free advertising by being creative.

Print advertising is one of the most expensive means of advertising, although Internet ads are increasing in price as this is becoming a more popular advertising medium. There are so many types of print media opportunities available for you. When seeking out opportunities, keep your Return on Investment (ROI) of time, money, and energy in mind to help you make good decisions.

Here are a few ideas for you to think about before making your decision about print advertising:

- Be prepared to advertise with some regularity. A one-off ad has very little impact. Keep repeating the ad and, over time, it will start to penetrate the readers' minds. An ad needs to be seen between 7 and 12 times before it is effective.

- Local newspapers are a great place to advertise and smaller magazine publications can give you a great ROI.

- Directories, Super Pages, and Yellow Pages are examples of different types of listings you can choose from. Paper directories are losing their popularity so I suggest that you look at some online directory advertising as well. If you do live in a smaller community, it may make sense for you to do paper ads in local directories, Yellow Pages, or magazines.

- National home decor or home staging magazines can be great places to advertise if you are looking for national or regional exposure. You need to have a very healthy budget for advertising in bigger magazines.

- Trade shows or conferences also offer the opportunity for print advertising in flyers and marketing materials.

If you want your brand to be recognized on a more national or global basis, then using the Internet will probably be more cost-effective than print ads. The following are some ideas for Internet advertising:

- You can do Internet ads with Google or Yahoo!, and purchase Internet ads such as the pay-per-click type, which show up at the top of the search engine findings page or along the sides. You need to determine which advertising scenario is best for you. Typically most start-up home stagers look at this option down the road when they have a larger advertising budget.

- *Real Estate Weekly* or home improvement Internet magazines or blogs are good targets and worth researching.

When you are first starting your business it is not likely that you will even have a media kit but in time you can build one through your articles, radio and television interviews, blog posts, and other media exposure you receive. As your business grows you may decide you would like to hire a public relations or media professional who can assist you in gaining greater publicity than if you were doing it on your own.

3.1 Article submissions

One of the most cost-effective methods of advertising your home staging business is to write articles for print and online. Do some Internet searches for electronic home staging articles and follow up with the sources that you come across. Think about all of the industry-related resources that would be interested in using current home staging articles.

When you are searching the Internet for interesting home staging articles, consider submitting some of your own articles to these sites. Articles written by you or about you keep your name out there so people are seeing you in a few different places and are starting to get to know you. You will build a reputation as being a "home staging expert," which is what you want. Remember potential clients need to see something about you, or something repeated 7 to 12 times, so this is another way to meet those numbers.

If you are not a natural writer, you may feel inspired by reading other people's articles. You can always do something as simple as writing a response to a blog or an article in the paper. If you are really not good at writing, consider investing in a great copywriter who can put your ideas into words for you. In your networking activities it is highly likely that you will meet a copywriter.

These are a few ideas for you to consider about your articles:

- Submit your article to as many places as you can; it doesn't matter how many places your article shows up.

- For magazines or newspaper submissions it is best to contact the editor. Approach this person with your idea from the perspective of what the publisher's readers will find most interesting and of value. Think like a reader.

- Look for industry-related websites, magazines, newspapers, and blogs where your home staging topic would offer value to their readers.

- Consider having a magazine or newspaper write an article about you — from a career angle or real estate staging business. It is worth noting that if you are being interviewed, some of the things written in the article may not be 100 percent accurate. Keep in mind the old adage "any publicity is good publicity."

- Most of the real estate staging articles to date contain before and after pictures, so make sure you have some good ones available to send in with an article because the publisher may ask for more.

- You always need to get permission to take photos of your clients' homes. All of the professional home-staging courses provide forms for this. You can find a Client Consent form (Form 2) on the CD.

- Proofread your articles and check over your pictures carefully to ensure you like the final edit. Although it is not always possible, ask if you can see the article before it goes to print.

- When you are doing your ezine or e-newsletter think about whom your target market audience is; what will be of interest to them and add value?

- Many networking groups offer their members the opportunity to write articles for a monthly ezine or newsletter. This is a fantastic way to get exposure while promoting you and your business. People will start to remember you through your articles.

✔ Be versatile with your topic as it is likely you could write about many things that would be of interest to a variety of readers.

3.2 Media releases

A media release (formerly called a press release) is a piece of "newsworthy" information that is sent to the media. A media release is always written in the third person. There are many resources to send your media releases to, so decide which ones you have a good chance of getting your release published. Note that the media is inundated with press releases and will only select those that they think are of special interest.

Here is something that I discovered about media releases:

✔ If you are doing some work with a charity, these types of announcements are more likely to go in the paper than ones promoting your business. There are some media that like to write about new entrepreneurs and changing careers or unusual careers. Your new home staging business would be a good fit for these types of media.

✔ Send media releases as often as you like without being obnoxious.

✔ Media releases usually go to the editor so look up that person's contact information and send the media release to him or her, then follow up with a phone call.

✔ If you really want to get someone's attention, send along a small gift so that you separate yourself from the others.

3.3 Other creative advertising ideas

There are other creative ways to advertise such as the following:

✔ **Bus or bench advertising:** This type of advertising is often a favorite among realtors. This can be a costly way to advertise yet it has been proven to be an effective strategy. Due to the investment in this type of advertising it might be something to look at in the future once you have built up your business brand.

✔ **Vehicle signs:** This is a relatively inexpensive way and considered a good investment for a start-up home staging business. There are two types of vehicle signs:

• Magnetic car signs: These can be made to fit the side panels of your vehicle. Most signage companies will make the signs for you with the input from your graphic designer or design the sign themselves. You are limited to the size and the amount of information you can get on a magnetic sign so consider having your company name, phone number, and website URL most prominent. This is a great idea if you are leasing a vehicle or want to take the signs off occasionally.

• Vinyl car graphics: Another great way to advertise is with vinyl graphics. This is a fabulous marketing strategy especially when the letters and graphics are large enough to read from a distance. You should have your company name, phone number, and website URL displayed prominently. Some people even have their graphics positioned so someone looking into his or her rear view mirror can read them. You can get your entire vehicle covered, or just sections of it.

- ✓ **Radio ads:** Radio ads can be quite costly versus some other forms of advertising. You need to buy repetitive ads; just like in print ads, the ad should air 7 to 12 times to make the investment worthwhile. You can also buy radio time where you are interviewed as the home staging expert for a call-in talk show. (**A word of caution:** Be wary of the television or radio show that wants to promote you for a price. Radio shows are very costly investments. This is something you can think of once you grow your business.) If you live in a small town, radio ads have proven to be effective since there is a smaller audience listening to the one station. If you live in a larger city, you will need to research to find out which radio stations your target market listens to.

- ✓ **Advertorials:** These are quite popular and often take up a half to a full page in a magazine or newspaper. These are intended to look like a news story rather than an ad that you are paying for. When these are done well it looks like the article was written *about* you and not *by* you! While they can be costly you can submit the advertorial to many websites that might want an article on home staging.

4. Presentations

Presentations are a terrific way to market your business at very little cost while having the potential of a much larger return if someone hires you for a home staging job because he or she heard you speak! Once you are somewhat established you will be building your portfolio as well as your confidence to be able to talk about what you do.

Doing a talk such as "How to prepare your house for selling" is a great topic and likely to attract many home sellers. Something that I have discovered from many of my talks is that a lot of the so called "do-it-yourselfers" (DIY) have great intentions but often call in professional stagers. They realize they cannot do all the work themselves or they do not really want to! Naturally they will think of you and your talk and want to hire you!

Make sure that at all of your presentations you get the names of the people who attended. The fortune is really in the follow-up so you need to ensure you have something to follow up on! One of the easiest and least intimidating ideas is to put a newsletter sign-up sheet on a clipboard and have people sign up for your free newsletter. You need to mention that by signing up for this newsletter people are giving you permission to add them to your mailing list. Many database systems will allow you to enter up to a certain number of names into your database and some will also then send an email requesting that the person *approve* that he or she wants to be on your mailing list.

On your newsletter sign-up sheet, put the heading at the top and then three columns (see Sample 2). Print or write in the names as samples because people will always copy what is written first! Ask them to write legibly so you can ensure they get your fantastic information-packed newsletter. I often put the name of the event at the bottom so I can remember where the names came from.

4.1 Different types of venues for public talks

There are numerous possible places for you to talk about the benefits of home staging. You will need to do some research to find out when talks are given and who to contact about doing

SAMPLE 2
NEWSLETTER SIGN-UP SHEET

Sign up for My Newsletter Full of Tips on Home Staging		
Note that by signing this form, and giving your contact information, you are giving me permission to add you to my company's mailing list.		
Name	**Phone**	**Email Address**
Susan Smith	555.555.5555	Susan@hotmail.com
William Doe	555-555-4444	WDoe@abccompany.com
Event: Home Staging Talk at the library on June 5, 20--		

a talk on home staging. If you have other topics you can talk about, you may be able to talk at several different venues which will help get your name out there.

The following are some of the more likely venues that would welcome your presentation:

  ↳ Libraries are a good place to do a public talk. Note that you should research the books available beforehand as the library will want you to reference some of these to its patrons.

  ↳ Real estate companies have weekly meetings where you can make a presentation.

  ↳ Many networking groups look for speakers.

  ↳ Retail stores often have workshops and want speakers.

  ↳ Many industry-related home decor stores such as furniture and even consignment stores often have speakers or weekend workshops free to their customers.

  ↳ Trade shows are often looking for topics of interest for their attendees. Home and

garden and real estate trade shows are two good venues to consider.

  ↳ Private groups such as church groups, clubs, and charities often look for guest speakers at their monthly meetings.

In order to make a great presentation you need to know your content inside and out, have visuals that can be easily seen by your audience and provide some type of handout that has your contact information on it. After all, the whole point of marketing yourself is so that people will know who you are and think of you first when they need a home stager.

4.2 Types of presentations

You may choose to do either a PowerPoint presentation or a more informal one that warrants different types of manual visual aids to support your presentation.

4.2a PowerPoint presentations

A PowerPoint presentation is the most professional way to make your presentation but might not be the most appropriate for the size of your

SAMPLE 3
POWERPOINT PRESENTATION

My TOP 5 SECRET SELLER TIPS
to sell for top dollar and quickly!

1. Declutter and depersonalize

2. Paint in a neutral color

3. Invest in new flooring

4. Update your lighting fixtures

5. Create lots of open space

audience. You need to have at least 20 people or more and be able to adjust the lighting in the room or area so your slides show well.

Many facilities have laptops and LCD projectors so that you do not need to invest in these yourself unless you want to. For your talk all you need to do is bring your information on a memory stick and download your presentation. Always give yourself plenty of time before your audience arrives to set everything up and ensure the equipment is working properly.

Let's pretend you are doing a library talk. Your first PowerPoint slide would have your logo, name, and the title of your talk on it. You would keep this up until you begin your talk. Be friendly, greet people, and get the first row of listeners engaged.

Keep your talk short and sweet and name it something that is going to get the sellers' attention. It might look something like Sample 3.

You would support each point with lots of your best before-and-after photos with limited text for each point.

I use this rule of thumb to determine the number of slides I need to have for a Power-Point presentation: *one slide per one minute*. This timing guideline has worked well over the years for me and just in case I finish up before my allotted time I always put in a few extra slides.

You want to be entertaining enough that your audience becomes very engaged and asks a lot of questions either during or at the end of your presentation.

4.2b Manual presentations

Manual presentations can take on a variety of forms. You may choose to have some large foam core boards made with your before-and-after photos on them. You can get these made at any office supply store that does copying and laminating. A good size for a smaller audience is a board that is approximately two feet by three feet and, of course, in color.

You may decide to provide laminated, color handouts for your audience with before and after photos on them so they have something they can view up close. Make sure you pick these up at the end of your presentation to use again.

In any opportunity where you have a captive audience, do a draw for something they would love to win, and follow up with everyone who entered your draw. It's always good to provide your audience with a handout so they have your contact information. It could be your business card, postcard, or flyer.

As was mentioned previously, it is vital that you follow up with your attendees. Otherwise, why do the talk in the first place? Create an entry form with areas for the potential clients to fill in their names, phone numbers, and mailing and email addresses. Have an area for them to select what they are interested in knowing more about, such as a color consultation, decluttering, decorating tips, getting ready to sell, and design updating. Make sure you have pens nearby so they can fill in this information.

4.2c Office realtor talks

Office realtor talks are one of the best strategies to include in promoting your home staging business. Almost all real estate companies hold weekly meetings for the realtors who are connected to their company. Larger real estate offices can have up to 200 or more realtors. However, generally only a small portion of realtors show up for the weekly in-house meetings for a variety of reasons. Some may be too busy getting clients or may not find the information of value to them.

It is a good idea to do some research before arriving to give your presentation. Research your targeted real estate office by going to its website to find out about the company and to see the realtors who are connected with the company.

Your first step in being invited to do a home staging presentation is to contact the office manager to set up an appointment. If you happen to already be working with a few of the realtors in the office you are targeting, mention that to the office manager as it just might be what you need to get your foot in the door!

When you have the opportunity to make a presentation at a real estate company's weekly meeting, make it short and to the point. Often, real estate offices will request that you keep your presentation to a certain time limit, which can be anywhere between 15 to 45 minutes.

You may or may not be able to do a Power-Point presentation due to the time constraints of the meetings, size of the group, or lighting restraints. If you are not doing a PowerPoint presentation then the manual way of using the foam core with before and after photos works well, along with your handout about your talk.

You can put your presentation materials together in a folder that is the same color as your branding, or simply use postcards and attach your business card to them. Leave some extra handouts and marketing materials for those realtors who were not able to be there. Often you can put those materials in the absent realtor's inbox in the office.

Always do a free draw for the attendees. You can make it a free one-hour home staging consultation or you can offer a free one-day home staging job. Follow-up is essential to your business and none more so than when you are meeting many realtors at one time. By asking them to put their business cards in for your free draw you will have the names of the attendees of your talk. You can follow up with each realtor by a phone call or send him or her a personalized automated ecard or paper card (e.g., from SendOutCards).

Your presentation should be supported with great before-and-after photos as well as with testimonials from realtors and clients. You can use your props and also provide the attendees with a one- or two-page handout covering your topics. Of course you should also provide them with your business card, postcard (if you have one), flyer, and some notes on your talk.

REALTOR PRESENTATION

TOP 5 REASONS TO WORK WITH A HOME STAGER

Does making money and getting referrals matter to you?

1. Expert Real Estate Agent + Expert Stager = Sold Property

2. Home stager services

3. Clients know what they need to do

4. "WOW" factor sells these homes

5. My credentials and why you should work with me!

Make your talk interesting, informative, and use your best before-and-after photos indicating what you did to make homes look so great. When you are creating your talk think about what results the realtors want to get from having a relationship with you.

Your opening talk slide might look like Sample 4. Use the version on the CD to develop the key points for your presentation.

For many realtors and sellers, statistics are very important. You need to ensure that you have either your own great statistics supporting positive home staging results, or source them from the Real Estate Staging Association's website, or via surveys for real estate professionals and homeowners at HomeGain.

Realtors like to know just how fantastic your work is as a home stager. They will want to know how long a property was on the market before it sold (i.e., before and after it was staged), if that applies; how many staged homes received their asking price (or more than the asking price); and what it cost to stage the home.

4.3 Paying workshops

Once you feel confident in your business success and your speaking skills you may want to start doing seminars or workshops for the general public and charging a small fee for them. It's best to use this formula to gauge when to start charging for your talks: free, free, *fee*, free, free, *fee*, etc.

There are several available venues that will give you great exposure while they do all the marketing for you! You can also promote your talks on your website. Consider contacting the program coordinators of community centers and schools.

There are a few things you need to know before you do a paying workshop:

- Your talks can be anywhere from a few hours to a full day of presenting.

- You can do a PowerPoint presentation or a manual talk.

- Have handouts available along with your contact information. Some programs have restrictions around how much self-promotion you can do so it is best to ask before signing up as a workshop presenter.

✓ Community centers are a great place to start. They often do a 50/50 or 60/40 split (60 percent to you) with the money collected from the attendees. Many community centers start their planning a full season or two ahead because they need to get information for their programs ready for the printer way in advance of the seminars and workshops they are offering. Contact them early enough so you won't be disappointed. Programs can be canceled based on not securing a minimum number of attendees. If that happens, don't worry, because your information still went out in their flyer and many people keep those around for a while.

✓ School boards offer not-for-credit courses to the general public. The pay rate and the cost of the seminar or workshop will vary across the country depending on your skill set and the perceived value of the course for the target market.

✓ You will be asked to submit a seminar description, the cost of the seminar, the minimum number of students you require, and supplies and equipment needed.

✓ Arrive early and be prepared to stay after your talk to answer more questions. This is where you will get some interested clients!

5. Trade Shows

In your community it is highly likely that there will be either real estate trade shows or home and garden trade shows that you can participate in as a home stager. Many women's networking groups hold trade shows throughout

the year that you can become involved with as well.

Trade shows are usually held for two to three days and often during the weekend when more people can attend. Booths range in price from a few hundred dollars to several thousand dollars depending on the type of booth set up, the location of your booth, and the booth-specific requirements.

The following are some helpful tips for when you are considering a booth at a trade show:

✓ Do your research first to find out if the trade show is going to attract your perfect clients (i.e., home sellers, realtors, and builders).

✓ If the trade show is more than a half day, make sure you have some help so that you can take bathroom and food breaks throughout the day.

✓ If you are sharing the cost of the booth, make sure you are clear on who will get the leads as the attendees approach people in the booth, and who will follow up.

✓ Wear comfortable shoes and bring two pairs so you can give your feet a break.

✓ Stage your booth so that it makes a "WOW" statement by setting up a vignette of a living room or bedroom. If you do not have your own staging inventory, rent some furnishings that draw attention to your booth. This is why your branding is so important. You want people to identify you by your branding and to remember who you are. Flowers always add an elegant touch to your booth and many women love to see them.

✓ Have plenty of wrapped candy available, and small giveaways such as nail files or measuring tapes (items with your logo on them).

- Have lots of business cards on hand to give away, and/or rack cards. All your marketing materials need to be coordinated and make your business stand out in the crowd.

- Having a large roll-up banner in your booth is a good way to attract attention and advertise your services. A good size for a banner is three feet by seven feet as that size stands out best. This is a much more cost-effective way than paying for a booth to be made up for you that can cost upward of $5,000.

- Have a free draw for your home staging services whether it is a one-hour consultation or as generous as a whole day home staging job. If this is not a business trade show, there might not be a lot of business cards on the patrons so you will need to have draw forms that people can fill out and drop in the draw box.

- Follow up from everyone who entered your draw and introduce yourself to them. As has been mentioned a few times already, follow-up is key; otherwise, why go through the expense of time, money, and energy in doing a trade show if you do not follow up to get clients?

Just like what was mentioned in section **4.2b** earlier, create an entry form with areas for the potential clients to fill in names, phone numbers, and mail and email addresses. Have an area on the form for them to select what they are interested in knowing more about such as a color consultation, decluttering, decorating tips, getting ready to sell, or design updating.

Many trade shows are looking for guest speakers. For example, I contacted the speaker committee chair and provided a brief description of what I wanted to talk about. This gave me extra exposure with my booth and my talk was promoted in the event's flyer!

Tip: If you have not entered the trade show, make up information packages that you can take around to the realtors who have booths and introduce yourself to them. The only investment here is some money for your marketing materials and your time versus the expense of a booth and your time in the booth!

6. Auctions and Golf Tournaments

Nonprofit organizations and public companies often have golf tournaments and fundraising events. Many of these events look for donations from sponsors or companies such as your home staging company, in the form of a product or service that their guests can bid on or buy.

You may want to consider the following tips:

- Offer a "Free One-Hour Staging Consultation" or a "Free One-Day Home Staging." Indicate the full value of the prize (i.e., a high hourly rate and a high rate for the entire day of staging).

- There is no limit to what you can offer — be creative; have a prize for everyone such as a free half-day staging consultation working with the home seller, or a $50 off coupon.

- Offer gift certificates of $100, or $100 off. See if these can be put in the goody bags that are often part of the auctions or tournaments.

- Find out if you can set up a nice table display or provide some promotional material for the promoters to use on the event's website or print material.

✔ Take some photos of you promoting your products at the events. This is great for your website and marketing materials.

7. Open Houses

In 2010, the National Association of Realtors (NAR) in the United States indicated that many realtors are no longer conducting open houses as one of their marketing tactics. This may be as a result of the downturn in the economy for this time period.

In Canada, this is not the case. You can make some great contacts at open houses, so look for them in your area. Go in and introduce yourself to the realtor or assistant as long as he or she is not busy with a potential buyer. Ask to set up an appointment with the realtor. This will give you another opportunity to meet with the person again. The realtor needs to get to know you, like you, and trust you before he or she will work with you.

7.1 Realtor open houses for home buyers

Many realtors that you have done staging jobs for will allow you to leave your marketing materials on the counter in the kitchen or at the front entrance of homes they are selling. Some realtors will also allow you to be present during the open house. Clipping your business card to your postcard or rack card and leaving it with a small giveaway such as an introductory coupon may just get you some business!

7.2 Realtor open houses for realtors

Realtors often have what is called a "realtor's open house" or an "agent's open house." This gives other realtors from different real estate companies the opportunity to come and take a look at the property to see if they might have an interested client.

You may be able to ask the realtor if you could meet the other realtors, or have the realtors go off for a few hours and then ask them to come back after you have staged the house. It's not a bad idea to entice them with some cookies and coffee for their efforts! Depending on how many realtors come back to see the transformation, you will have converted those who do not yet believe in home staging into believers. They will be excited to work with you to see how you can help their clients. For the already converted you will gain some new connections who you can follow up with.

7.3 Other realtors' open houses

It is a great idea to go to as many open houses in your area as you can. Go in and introduce yourself and ask to follow up with them. If you think the home could use a home stager make sure you ask them if they had the home staged. They might have done it themselves so listen to their response before you say anything.

As was mentioned earlier, if the realtor is too busy, request a meeting with him or her and acknowledge that you do not want to take up his or her time as getting this property sold is the realtor's main priority!

8. Retail Locations for Promoting Your Business

Many retail stores are perfect marketing venues to introduce your home staging business to. Here are some ideas but do not limit yourself to this list of where you can market your home staging business.

8.1 Fitness centers or gyms

Many fitness clubs will allow you to put up a flyer or poster with your contact information. The only requirement is that you will need to get the flyer or poster approved by the manager of the center. Typically you can leave flyers up for a month. Consider changing your content every season and offer specials throughout the year.

Some clubs and centers will invite you to do a free draw each month. Larger organizations have a "customer appreciation night" to which they invite sponsors and customers. As a home stager you could provide a gift or coupon for your services.

8.2 Home decor stores

Many small, privately owned home decor stores will allow you to come and do a short workshop about what you have to offer. Most store alliances expect that their customers would buy some of their product that you are promoting in your talk (e.g., furniture stores, lighting stores, art stores, etc.).

You could also leave flyers with a special introductory offer, or your business card stapled to with your postcard or rack card.

8.3 Coffee shops and restaurants

Many coffee shops and casual restaurants have dedicated areas to allow their customers to promote their businesses. Some have bulletin boards where you can put up your flyer or an area where you can leave your business cards. Think about leaving something with a promotional offer and a call to action. Make sure your flyer has tear-away strips with your contact information so that people can take this information with them.

In some cities there is a publication called *Coffee News* or *Coffee Club News* that you can advertise in for your area.

9. Television

There are opportunities for you to be on television even if you do not have your own television show. There are many new television shows in the works for home staging. If you have an idea, you can present it to the production manager and see if you can sell him or her on your idea. You can call television producers to see if they feel your idea is worth talking about. Many home stagers have been on television in short news segments and on shows promoting women in business.

8
Marketing Tools

Now that you know the *how*, *where*, and *when* strategies, we are going to look at the *what* marketing tools you will use when applying your strategies.

I cannot stress enough how important it is to spend money on hiring professionals to do some of your marketing materials, especially if you have never started a business before. If you cannot afford to hire someone in the beginning, make sure that if you are creating your own marketing materials that they at least look professional. Since you are going to be charging professional rates for a professional service, everything about you needs to be professional!

In the home staging profession, you never get a second chance to make a great impression. This rule also applies when you meet new people. Take your time developing your materials to ensure they represent your brand and reflect who you are — a home staging professional.

1. Promotional Materials — Print

Your print materials will come in many shapes and sizes and they all represent your brand. You will find that you use some of your print marketing pieces more than others.

1.1 Business cards

Your business card is often the first marketing material you use to introduce yourself. Many times your business card is the only marketing piece you will carry with you and it should be carried with you at *all* times. I cannot stress this enough. As a home stager you will be meeting people all the time and sometimes networking in what may seem like the most unlikely places, such as waiting in a store lineup!

You will need to spend a lot of time on research to help you decide on your business name, tagline, logo, and color scheme which will represent you and your brand on your business card. Here are some suggestions to consider when investing in your new business cards:

- You can engage the services of a graphic artist for the design of your cards. This may also be part of a service your webmaster or a printing company offers. It may be an hourly rate or part of a package. Get three quotes from different designers and printers for your business cards.

- Use both sides of the card since the back is considered "wasted real estate" if you do not use it.

- Keep some white space on your card for people to make notes if they want to. Some home staging business cards have appointment information on the back much like you would see on an appointment card from a doctor or dentist's office.

- Use good quality paper such as heavy stock at 14- or 15-point and have the cards printed on an "offset" printer versus a digital one for a better quality image.

- If you are into eco-friendly products, you can get your business cards printed on recycled paper; some can be made glossy.

- If you are making your own business cards, ensure they have a professional look. If you are using a template, spend the extra money to do both sides.

- Some people like to put their photo on their cards and others will use their logo. Note that people will remember your logo or your face more than your name or the name of your company.

- A graphic designer will know the best fonts to use to represent your brand. (My cards have Charlotte Sans font in both uppercase and lowercase letters.)

- Your name and phone number should be in a larger font than the name of your company.

- It is important to have a tagline. A tag line explains more about your business or is a catchy phrase describing the benefit of using your services. My first company was "Sun on My Back Redesigns" and my tagline was "Remember … the way you LIVE in your HOME, is not the way you SELL your HOUSE!"

- It is not essential that your card has your address on it but if you have a website and/or fax number, these should be on the card. You can also use a post office box number. If you have a home-based business, using a post office box ensures that no one will be making unexpected visits to your home; it will mean that strangers won't know where you live as this can be a safety issue.

- There are many free or low-cost template business cards sites that you can find on the Internet. A word of caution is that you always get what you pay for. When you are just starting out you do not need to do everything all at once. However, your business card will be one of your most used marketing tools. Some stagers start out by using Vistaprint, which is an inexpensive website that can produce your cards.

- To get you started in your research for your business card, complete Exercise 12 to find out your likes and dislikes. Collect six business cards that you like.

EXERCISE 12
BUSINESS CARDS: YOUR LIKES AND DISLIKES

Business card company name	Something you like about the card and why you like it	Something you do not like about the card and why	Which traits would you incorporate for your brand?

Indicate why you like them and which traits you would like as part of your brand.

1.2 Postcards and rack cards

Postcards and rack cards have replaced brochures as key marketing tools in the home staging business. Postcards are usually four inches by six inches while rack cards are typically four inches by nine inches and are made to stand up on racks or rack displays.

Here are a few suggestions when designing your postcard or rack card:

- ✔ To be consistent with your overall brand, give the cards the same look as your website in terms of the logo, colors, and message.

- ✔ You can put more information on the cards because they are larger than your business card so make sure you utilize the space.

- ✔ Use the *best* before-and-after photos of your work.

- ✔ You can change your tagline and add more benefit statements to your message.

- ✔ Promote your services using bullet points.

- ✔ Use lots of white space with clear contact information.

- ✔ Use client testimonials — short and sweet, and ones that praise your work.

- ✔ You may want to use a "call to action" on your postcard or rack card or you may save this to put on a flyer with some kind of special offer or coupon discount.

1.3 Flyers

Flyers can be easily done if you have your own software graphics package such as Microsoft Publisher, or you can hire a graphic artist to do them for you. Most people use flyers to promote something, perhaps a "special" with a coupon discount. If you do print your rates on your materials, make sure you keep them current.

When you are deciding on what kind of flyer to create remember that color printing costs much more than black and white. Having said that, color pictures do show up better. If you didn't use color, you could attach your business card and/or postcard to add some color to the flyer.

If you are doing a single flyer or just a few, then it is best to make color copies using great before-and-after photos along with testimonials. Many fitness and community centers, and stores, will allow you to post flyers with their approval for a limited time period. Make sure you offer a way for clients to contact you. You can put perforations or cut the bottom of your flyer in sections so prospects may easily tear off your contact information. If possible, you could make a pouch for your business cards or, if allowed, leave a stand displaying your business cards near the flyer.

If you are printing lots of flyers, using colored paper will be the less expensive route to go. Use large fonts with a "call to action" to create a sense of urgency and include an expiry date. You can use these as inserts in newsletters and newspapers, and distribute them in whole neighborhoods doing a postal code drop. Check out your post office to see how you can get your flyers in with their mail drops.

You can also drop off of your flyer at real estate agents' offices.

1.4 Brochures

Brochures tend to go out of date sooner than other marketing materials and there is more text and visuals on them that need updating. If you create brochures, be more generic than specific so they will be usable for a longer period of time.

Three-fold brochures are quite effective and can be done with many software packages if you want to design your own. As long as it looks professional then do it; if not, hire a professional graphic artist to do it for you. An e-brochure can obviously be changed more often and is therefore more cost-effective.

1.5 Greeting cards

Greeting cards are excellent tools for following up and keeping in touch with clients. Fortunately with today's technology you can actually send automated greeting cards from your computer or, if you prefer, you can hand write and hand mail cards. Either way, cards are one of the best, most personal ways to keep in touch with your clients. Emails are good for communicating but we all get too many of those!

SendOutCards was one of the first companies to come up with the idea of being able to choose a paper card online, customize it, and then have it put in an envelope and mailed for you. You can also send gifts or gift cards (e.g., coffee cards for Starbucks or Tim Hortons, books, food such as brownies and cookies, or baby gifts) with SendOutCards and never have to leave your desk to do it! This is a very cost-effective and time-saving way to send cards to anyone.

1.6 Portfolio

Your portfolio will consist of your visuals, being your best before-and-after photos, along with "raving fan" testimonials. It is a great idea to show photos of rooms you have transformed, as well as photos of small vignettes that captivate the eye because of their beauty. If you have done other home-staging related work, use these photos to accurately portray all the work you have done, and what you could do for the prospect or client.

You can make a stand alone portfolio by creating a scrapbook of your successes and then use this on your sales calls.

Another way to show your portfolio is to create a hard copy book. This can be done through photo stores or online. One company I have used is Shutterfly and the cost was about $60, which is a great investment. This can also be used for other presentations. Hard copies work well if left on a table at a trade show booth.

1.7 Marketing binder

There are many different types of binders that you can select to house your marketing materials. Select a nice professional-looking binder that represents you and your business. If there is one in your branding colors, all the better!

Keep your binder clean and simple so that nothing falls out when you open it. The binder could contain but is not limited to the following:

- Business cards
- Postcards, rack cards, or flyers (materials you will leave)
- A pad of lined paper (clean sheets)
- Pen
- Your best before-and-after photos (if you do not have a separate portfolio)
- Testimonials
- Any forms that you need to use in your presentation
- Industry-related articles that you have or someone else has written
- Other related forms for your specific sales call

1.8 File or presentation folders

There will be times that you will want to put together some information to leave with your prospective client. Typically you will put this in file folders or presentation folders. If you are meeting with a lot of people and doing a presentation, you can decide whether the file folder look is appropriate or if it is better to use a glossy presentation folder.

Your budget does factor in what type of folder you leave your prospect or client. You can use colored folders that are in your brand color, recycled paper folders, or the classic black presentation folder. Always keep in mind the image you want your business's brand to portray and remember how important that first impression is!

In a folder for a realtor or home seller you might include:

- Business card
- Postcard, rack card, or other marketing materials
- List of your services in bullet form
- List of service fees exclusively for them
- Any articles that support real estate staging such as statistics you have found on the Internet or recent newspaper or magazine articles
- Testimonials
- Small giveaways such as a nail file or note pad
- Special offer, gift certificate, or discount coupon

1.9 Direct mail campaigns

Direct mail campaigns can be very effective ways to market your business and cost-effective if you go through your federal postal system. However, with this type of marketing piece you will not be able to follow up with your prospects, they will need to follow up with you. Remember, you need to repeat a message between 7 and 12 times for people to respond to your information.

That said, if you have the budget for this, it can be a great marketing strategy and tool.

In the United States you can go online to United States Postal Service and search the site under "Direct Mail" to get the information you require to proceed with your campaign. There are maps and areas that you can select for your campaign.

In Canada you can go online to Canada Post's website and look under "Business," then "Residential and Business Counts and Maps." Currently, you can either do your own flyer (which needs to meet Canada Post's mailing requirements) or they will do one for you at a higher cost than if you created your own. You determine what postal codes you want your material to go to and provide it to Canada Post who will deliver it for you. This is a popular marketing method for realtors!

You can design your own piece or work with a graphic artist. It can be a postcard or a flyer that you put in an envelope. Some components to a great direct-mail marketing campaign include:

- Know who you are targeting and why you have selected them.

- Use a WIFM ("what's in it for me") catchy headline to grab the reader's attention.

- Indicate what you are selling — special offer or percentage off.

- Use short client testimonials.

- Include a "call to action."

- Make it easy to contact you.

- Include a PS (postscript) as these are almost always read.

- You need to determine your timeline as to when you will send the next piece of mail to your prospects.

2. Promotional Materials — Electronic

Today, computers and the Internet play significant roles in both our personal and professional lives. As a home stager you will be using the Internet as one of your key marketing strategies and tools to promote your business. You do not have to be proficient in using software packages but you do need to have some basic knowledge of how to send emails and to respond to them. You can hire professionals to create some of your electronic marketing materials if you cannot do the work yourself.

2.1 Website

Almost all businesses now require a website presence on the Internet. The first thing most people do after they meet you is to check out your website to gain more information about you. Not having a website can leave your contacts with a negative opinion about you and your business. They may think you are just starting out, that you only do this part time, and that you are not a professional. While the first two statements may be true your clients do not need to know this. Perception is everything! Remember that someone coming to your website for the first time is creating his or her own "first impression" of you and your business. Think about how important your website is going to be!

You can have a website built for you, buy a software package to help you design one yourself, or check out websites that you can build online. Prices have gone down considerably for creating websites. Microsoft FrontPage is an affordable and user-friendly option to create your own website.

In the beginning I made the mistake of hiring a relative to create my website. This person was knowledgeable about building websites and the price was right but the experience was not so good. When someone is building your website on the side, naturally he or she cannot dedicate the time that a professional would. During my years teaching home staging, I cannot tell you how many similar negative experiences my graduates have had who hired a friend or relative to do their websites. It either does not get done on time or it does not look the way you envisioned. Many times people feel they can't say too much about it because they don't want to hurt the designer's feelings, but in the end, the owner of the site is the one who has to live with it! When you hire a professional to work with, you can expect professionalism all the way.

You will need to budget money as well as time for your website. While your website needs to look professional in your first year, you do not need to have all the bells and whistles. You can change your website as your business grows along with your finances. You can pay to have your website "search engine optimized" (SEO) to increase traffic to it and/ or you can pay for sponsored links. There are many ways to get traffic to your website, including good referral links.

There are many basic costs that you will incur when setting up a website. You will need to select and pay for your domain name, pay for a host, and engage the services of a graphic designer or web designer. Costs for these services can range from $20 for six months for do-it-yourself websites, up to $2,000 (or more) for a professional to do it for you. If someone is offering to build your site for more than $3,000, I would caution that you do not need to invest that much at this time.

For many people starting out, consider having a website that you can make changes to rather than having your webmaster do it for you. If you are computer savvy, select a website pro-

gram that allows you to manage content. Called a Content Management System (CMS), it will allow you to make changes yourself so you don't always have to pay someone to do it. If you are not at all technically inclined, hiring a webmaster is a very good thing! As you build your portfolio the one thing you may change on a more regular basis will be your before and after photos.

The following are some options for inexpensive template websites:

- ✔ 1&1 (www.1and1.com): If you are technically inclined and you think you can build your own website, this is the place to check out.

- ✔ WebKRAVE (www.webkrave.com) is another site to check out for lower cost websites.

Some website designers who have done work for real estate staging or related businesses can be found by searching out your competitors' and collaborators' websites. To find the website company, look at the bottom of the site to see if it says who built it.

In Exercise 13, find three websites that you like. Find two things for each site that you like and one thing you do not like that creates the brand of the company. Explain why you like or don't like the branding.

Most staging websites contain five main pages with subpages:

- ✔ Home

- ✔ About Us — Who We Are

- ✔ Services Offered (e.g., real estate staging, move-in redesigns, decorating, color consultations, downsizing, etc.)

- ✔ Before-and-after Photos (e.g., gallery, or portfolio) with testimonials

- ✔ Contact Us

EXERCISE 13
WEBSITES: YOUR LIKES AND DISLIKES

Website URL	Something you like about the website and why you like it	Something you do not like about the website and why	Which traits would you incorporate for your brand?

In addition to these standard five pages you may want to consider starting a blog on your site. Ask your webmaster how you can link your company blog to your personal blog and other social networks so you only need to write one blog post that is posted to the other sites.

2.2 Social networks

Chapter 7 included information about social networking. Every day this type of marketing is increasing in popularity and should become one of your consistent marketing tools. Social media experts tell us to spend about 15 minutes per day communicating in our social networks.

As mentioned previously, blogs are becoming more and more popular for marketing a business, so link your blog to your social networking sites. You can also brag about how happy your clients were through testimonials and photos in your social networks.

2.3 Ezines and e-newsletters

Once you have your very first client you will want to enter his or her contact information into your database. In the beginning your database can be as simple as recording contact information in MS Outlook or whichever computer program you are using.

As your client list grows you will want to start writing a newsletter full of interesting information for your clients. Most people use an electronic newsletter rather than paper to send in the mail. This is called an ezine or e-newsletter. The best way to start growing your list is to have an ezine or e-newsletter sign-up button on the home page of your website. You might want to start with a monthly e-newsletter and then send e-newsletters for special promotions or seasonal offers of your services.

As you grow, set a goal to send out at least two ezines per month. Many professional marketing specialists suggest a weekly ezine is the best way to keep in touch with your market. In the beginning this may seem like a daunting task so just take your time, and remember your business is all about the pace you set for your success — it's not a race.

There are several software packages, such as Constant Contact and VerticalResponse, that you can purchase to manage your database and your output of electronic messages. For more information on resources go to eVision Media's website. Susan Friesen of eVision Media suggest using this outline for your ezine:

- Introduction
- Client showcase
- Your recommendations
- Feature article
- Your assignment
- Your bio/profile

Friesen also states that your ezine is not to be used as a form of advertising. It is a way of building your business and attracting your ideal client. Remember, it's all about people getting to know you, like you, and trust you. Provide them with a quality e-newsletter and you are on your way!

As you meet more people at networking events, trade shows, etc., you will start collecting business cards. Because of the privacy issues you will need to get people's permission to put them in your database. This is what is typically done electronically once you enter them into your database: the recipient will receive an email asking them to "accept" or "reject" the invitation to receive future mailings from you.

2.4 E-articles

If you like to write, or if you can afford to hire a ghost writer to market you through articles, there are many sites who are looking for home staging articles. The best way to find out where to submit your articles is by doing an Internet key word search using "home staging e-articles" as a start. You can then research further by clicking on the articles to find out where they are being posted.

Now that you have been introduced to numerous marketing strategies for your business, take some time to think about which ones you could implement and give yourself a deadline date to complete the implementations.

9
Start-up Costs and
Monthly Expenses

One of the great features of starting your home staging business is that it is relatively inexpensive compared to other start-up business ventures. Unless you are investing in a lot of big inventory you should not need to get a bank loan to get started.

Most people will not be able to just jump into a home staging business without worrying about being able to pay their existing and future bills. As suggested in Chapter 2, you should create a business plan to determine how and when you can afford to start your home staging business part or full time.

It is worth mentioning that women more than men tend to be "risk averse" and often will not make the required initial investment. If you are really serious about starting a home staging business, you will need several thousand dollars

to get started. Depending on which professional services you hire and how much marketing you do, your first year costs should be between $3,000 and $5,000. If you start using professional services immediately and join several networking groups right away then this cost may be higher. This estimated cost does not include inventory, so be sure to factor that in depending on what you intend to buy. Consider using your credit line or find other means to get the necessary start-up funds you will need.

1. Income

When starting up your new business it is important that you know what your income or revenues (money in) and your expenses (money out) will be. This can be somewhat challenging in your first year because you have nothing to base your ability to get sales on. However, you need to take a positive approach and believe that you can achieve the goals you set for yourself.

We will go into more detail about pricing your home staging services in Chapter 11 but for the meantime, let's take a look at a formula you can use to determine how much money you will need to make to comfortably pay your bills and live the lifestyle you want.

1.1 Calculating annual income to weekly income

It's easiest to work backwards when calculating your annual income to weekly income by looking at how much money you need to make in a 46-week year. Not many people in business actually work 52 weeks of the year so we need to account for vacation days, sick days, statutory holidays, and the unexpected things in life that take us away from our business. See Sample 5 for how to make your calculations.

Figure out your own weekly income by using Exercise 14.

1.2 Calculating monthly income from weekly income

You could calculate your monthly income by multiplying your weekly income goal x 3.83 (i.e., 46 weeks divided by 12) or whatever number of weeks you believe you will work in the year. See Sample 6 for how to determine your monthly income goal.

Use Exercise 15 to help determine your desired monthly income.

2. Standard Start-up Costs: Expenses

To start your home staging business there are some standard expenses that are mandatory to setting yourself up as a professional home stager. The following are examples of what you will need for printing, electronic materials, networking, office costs, banking charges, a vehicle, tools, and miscellaneous.

Naturally the prices quoted below will vary not only from city to city, but from country to country. The ranges are average prices in North America. Always shop around to get the best price. Get three quotes for work you are getting done professionally. The prices quoted here are for professional quality products or services in the mid-price range. I recommended that you do not get the least expensive products or services unless the quality is also there. Your marketing materials are your brand and everything you use represents your brand.

You will need the following print materials:

- ✔ Business cards: $60 to $125 (quantity: 500)

- ✔ Postcard or rack cards: $160 to $250 (quantity: 500)

- ✔ Brochures: $180 to $310 (quantity: 250)

Electronic materials include:

- ✔ Website: $200 for a do-it-yourself site (i.e., one that is a template provider)

- ✔ Website:* $1,500 for a very basic site that is professionally done and may include some branding, $2,500+ for a professionally done website which includes branding and other marketing materials

- ✔ Social networks: Free to set up unless your webmaster or graphic artist is setting up your social networks using your branding.

*Note: Your time is not being calculated with the do-it-yourself sites but when you are paying a professional, he or she is charging for the project and the person will definitely include his or her time.

SAMPLE 5
CALCULATING ANNUAL INCOME FROM WEEKLY INCOME

Example A

Annual goal is $10,000 part time
1. 52 weeks - 6 weeks (e.g., vacation, sick days, statutory holidays) = 46 weeks
2. $10,000 ÷ 46 = $217/week

Example B

Annual goal is $ 50,000 full time
1. 52 weeks - 6 weeks (e.g., vacation, sick days, statutory holidays) = 46 weeks
2. $50,000 ÷ 46 = $1,087/week

EXERCISE 14
DETERMINING YOUR DESIRED WEEKLY INCOME

	Annual Income Goal	Number of Weeks Working	Weekly Income Goal (Divide annual income by weeks)
Part Time	$		$
Full Time	$		$

You will need to consider networking fees in your start-up costs:

- Annual fee: $75 to $290

- Monthly fees: $0 to $30

- Event fees: $10 to $60 depending on the event

Don't forget your office costs:

- Furniture such as a desk and chairs: $100 to $700

- Computer: $500 to $2,000

- Printer, scanner, and fax machine: $60 to $180

- Cell phone: $50 to $100 per month depending on the phone plan

- Filing cabinet: $30 to $100

- Portfolio binder: $15 to $50

You will definitely need a work vehicle so make sure to include these costs:

- Leasing a vehicle: $150 to $500 per month

CALCULATING MONTHLY INCOME FROM WEEKLY INCOME

Example A

Weekly goal is $217/week part time
1. 52 weeks - 6 weeks (e.g., vacation, sick days, statutory holidays) = 46 weeks
2. $10,000 ÷ 46 = $217/week
3. $217 x 3.83 weeks/month = $831.11

Example B

Weekly goal is $1,087/week full time
1. 52 weeks - 6 weeks (e.g., vacation, sick days, statutory holidays) = 46 weeks
2. $50,000 ÷ 46 = $1,087/week
3. $1087 x 3.83 weeks/month = $4,163.21

EXERCISE 15
DETERMINING YOUR DESIRED MONTHLY INCOME

	Weekly Income Goal	Number of Weeks Working (You decide)	Monthly Income Goal (Multiply weekly income goal by number of weeks working)
Part Time	$		$
Full Time	$		$

✔ Purchasing a vehicle: $15,000 (or more)

You will need many tools for this business including, but not limited to, the following:

✔ Tool kit: $50 to $75

✔ Small dolly: $50 to $100

✔ Leverage enhancer: $20

✔ Three-step step ladder: $20 to $30

✔ Drill: $40 to $150

✔ Levels (2-inch to 24-inch): $10 to $20

✔ Laser level: $20 to $50

✔ Gliders, sliders, move alls (minimum two sets of each): $10 to $15 for a set of four

✔ Hammers (small and large): $20 to $35

✔ Retractable screwdriver: $20

- Small case to hold picture hangers and hooks: $10
- Picture hangers and hooks: $10 to $20
- Screws and wall anchors: $3 to $20 depending on number per box
- Sticky hooks: $3 each to $10 per package of three
- Box of one-inch nails: $5
- Picture wire: $2 to $5
- No-nail picture hangers: $3 to $10 per pack
- Felt pads in a variety of sizes: $2 to $10
- Measuring tape (self-centering Lufkin is best): $5 to $10
- Microfiber cloths: $5 to $10
- Jiffy wipes: $5 to $10 per bag or box
- Box of T.S.P. (Trisodium Phosphate cleaner): $2
- Masking tape: $2+
- Duct tape: $3+
- Painter's tape: $4+
- Large piece of fabric for table coverage: $10 to $20
- Mr. Clean Magic Eraser: $3+
- Artist's eraser: $3
- Utility or X-ACTO knife: $15 to $20
- Wire cutters: $10
- Scissors: $10
- String: $5
- Pliers (plain and needle nosed): $15
- Regular wrench and Allen wrench sets: $12
- Glue (Krazy Glue, China, White): $3
- PORC-a-FIX (for appliances and bathtubs): $6
- Glue gun: $10+
- Wite-Out correction fluid: $2 bottle
- HB Pencils: $5
- Furniture marking pens (variety of colors): $3 to $10 a pack
- No-scratch light or dark stain for hardwood scratches: $10 to $20 bottle
- Spackle and spackle knife: $5 to $15
- Hand-held vacuum: $30 to $40
- Steamer: $75 to $100
- Goo Gone: $5
- Stud finder: $15+
- Non-staining Sticky Tack: $3 per pack
- Tacks (push pins and thumb tacks): $3
- Hang & Level (picture hanging tool): $20
- Leverage Enhancer: $20
- Paper towels: $5
- Windex or Windex Wipes: $5
- Cable and telephone cords (10 to 25 feet): $10 to $25

There are also miscellaneous items you need such as the following:

- Business approval and registration: $40 to $100
- Business license: $100 to $150
- Camera: $200 to $750
- Business bank accounts: $0 monthly charges to $60 per month plus transaction fees depending on minimum monthly balance

There are a few items listed that you may decide you cannot afford at this time. Know that you can add anything to your business at any time as long as it makes sense as an expense.

In the beginning you may not have the funds to invest in professional services such as a graphic designer, webmaster, lawyer, trademark specialist, bookkeeper, accountant, or a business coach. As your business grows you will be able to hire professionals to take your business to the next level.

Costs for professional advice may include the following:

- Graphic designer: $50 to $100 per hour or per project
- Webmaster: $30 to $150 per hour or per project
- Lawyer: $150+ per hour
- Trademark specialist: $100+ project pricing
- Bookkeeper: $20 to $40 per hour
- Accountant: $100+ per hour
- Business coach: $100+ per hour

Exercise 16 will help you calculate your six-month income and expenses. As suggested earlier, you may not want to quit your current job until you have your desired income from your home staging business. While you are starting out it would be wise to look at your other income for the purpose of this exercise.

Each month you will have some fixed costs and over time you will be better able to see where you can afford to make new purchases as your business grows.

As your business grows you will also want to change *what* you do in your business. Eventually you will be delegating work that you did in the beginning because it will not make sense if you are making $75 an hour to be doing administrative work that you could pay someone $20 an hour to do. When you start a business "you are working *in* your business," and as it grows you get others to work in your business while you focus your attention on "working *on* the business" and taking it to the next level. Very often when you start your business you have created a "job" for yourself and, in time, following your business plan and goals you can create a business you can sell. If selling your business is one of your goals then keep that foremost in your mind as you make business decisions.

EXERCISE 16
SIX-MONTH WORKSHEET FOR INCOME VERSUS EXPENSES

Income/Revenues — A						
Source	1st Month	2nd Month	3rd Month	4th Month	5th Month	6th Month
Staging clients						
Other income						
Total Income — A						

Expenses — B						
Category	1st Month	2nd Month	3rd Month	4th Month	5th Month	6th Month
Advertising and marketing						
Bank charges						
Tools						
Office supplies						
Meals and entertainment						
Printing						
Subcontractor fees						
Website						
Automobile						
Insurance						
Bookkeeper						
Parking						
Professional fees						
Telephone						
Cell phone						
Licenses						
Networking and professional meetings						
Miscellaneous						
Total Expenses — B						

Total Income — A						
Total Expenses — B						
Subtract B from A Credit (+) or Debit(-)						

10
Services Offered by Home Stagers

There are some very standard home staging services that most home stagers will offer their clients when getting their homes ready for selling. The number and variety of services that you have to offer will depend on what skills you already possess and can confidently provide for your clients.

You will find all the necessary forms and reports you will need to accompany your service offerings in this and subsequent chapters of the book. You will also find the forms on the accompanying CD. In Chapter 11 you will find the pricing guidelines that accompany your service offerings.

1. Consultations

Knowing how to do a variety of home staging consultations is going to be the key to your

success with clients. Not every potential client that you meet with is going to be a good fit for you, and vice versa. It is at the initial meeting that you need to make the decision whether you will work together or not.

The biggest reason that home staging jobs can go sideways is when the client is not emotionally ready to sell the home. The second biggest reason is that potential clients *think* they know what the home should look like and do not agree with or follow all of your recommendations.

Consider the consultation much like you would an interview. It requires an exchange of information as well as educating the client on what home staging encompasses and what it does not.

The following is a typical consultation scenario:

- Phone and make an appointment with the seller. If this is a realtor referral, let the client know this.

- Before you meet with the client you will have entered the contact information of the client on the Client Consultation form. (See Form 1.)

- Find out as much as possible on the phone about what type of consultation the person is expecting and how long he or she wants you to spend with him or her. If the person doesn't know, offer him or her some options of a quick-look consultation (e.g., 15 to 30 minutes or more) or an in-depth consultation (e.g., two to three hours). This will also help you determine your charges later.

- Meet with the seller and/or realtor in the seller's home and discuss what your time with the seller will be about.

- Build rapport by taking a tour of the home, inside and outside, to see how much work needs to be done to prepare the house for selling.

- Go through the consultation form questions (see Form 1) to determine the services the seller needs to hire you for.

- The next steps will depend on the services selected by the seller:

  - It is most likely that you will have to give the seller homework before you can do your staging work.

  - If a quote is required, let the person know either the range of services you think it will cost or that you will get back to him or her with a proper quote delivered in person or by email.

  - Once the seller has engaged your services it is recommended that you get at least a 50 percent deposit depending on the time frame of the staging work to be done. For example, if you are staging the house the next week, you may forego getting the deposit and let the person know you expect payment when you have finished the staging work.

  - If you want to take before-and-after photos, and you want a testimonial, the seller will need to complete the Client Consent form. (See Form 2.)

1.1 Free consultations

Many stagers offer free one-hour consultations because they know other stagers in their area are doing this. If you are providing a consultation with expert advice, you can provide it for free; however, I encourage you to find something more of *value* that you could offer the client rather than not getting paid for your expertise. Perhaps the opportunity to sign up for your ezine or e-newsletter that offers great tips to home sellers and home dwellers, or an invitation to attend one of your workshops. Even though you may do these for free for the general public you are still providing something more than other stagers.

There are a few times when offering something free does make sense because you can upsell your services at another time. Try the following examples:

- If you wanted to do a quick-look consultation (e.g., 15 to 30 minutes) to see the property and meet the client before you decide whether or not you want to do the staging job, or if the person wants to work with you.

- At your networking groups, using your table display, you may want to have a draw for a "free one-hour consultation."

FORM 1
CLIENT CONSULTATION

Client Information

Name: _____ Date: _____

Address: _____ Zip or postal code: _____

Cross streets: _____

Home phone: _____ Cell phone: _____

Email: _____

Parking information: _____

Home Information

Age of house: _____ Square footage: _____

Last major updates: _____

Curb appeal rating: _____ Garage: _____

Number of rooms: _____ Bedrooms: _____

Number of levels in house: _____

Listing Information

If listed, MLS or website: _____ Number of days on the market: _____

Reasons for not selling: _____

Price reductions: $ _____ When: _____

If not listed, listing date: _____ Realtor: _____

List price: $ _____

Emotional Factors

How motivated are the sellers to sell: _____

Budget Information

Overall budget for improvements: $ _____

Home staging budget: $ _____

Preparation Required

Overall clutter: _____

Storage area: _____

Moving company contacted: _____

FORM 1 — CONTINUED

Knowledge of Home Staging Services

Home seller: _____

Realtor: _____

Home Staging Services Required

[   ] Color Consultation   [   ] Prepack/Organizing

[   ] Decluttering   [   ] Recommendation report

[   ] Shopping   [   ] Open house/Showing check-in

[   ] Rooms inventory required: _____

[   ] Home staging number of assistants required: _____

[   ] Destaging, if required: _____

Other Services Required

[   ] Painter   [   ] Contractor   [   ] Landscaper

[   ] Cleaners   [   ] Flooring company   [   ] General handyman

If Realtor or Client Is Requesting a Bid or Proposal from You

Who else is submitting a bid or proposal? _____

What criteria are you basing the successful bid or proposal on? _____

When will you make your final decision? _____

Do you have any concerns that I should be aware of? _____

Other Pertinent Information Required

_____

_____

Billing Information

Charges for (date): _____

Future charges: _____

Other: _____

Other

Take photos: _____

Follow-up date: _____

How did you hear about my company? _____

Enter client information into database: _____

FORM 2
CLIENT CONSENT

Photos and Testimonial Request

I give my permission and consent to _____ to take before and after photos,
(insert your company name)
being photographed of my home, to include the interior and exterior. I agree that the photos may
be used by _____ for certain marketing purposes such as being posted on the
(insert your company name)
company's website and other promotional and general marketing materials, provided that my full
name is not identified with any of the photos. I do agree that you may use my first name and my
location.

If I decide to provide a written testimonial, you may use or publish it for the same marketing
purposes as stated above.

Accepted By

Signature: _____

Print full name: _____

Date: _____

By doing this you get to add new people to your database with whom you can follow up.

You may decide to offer free one-hour consultations or one-day staging to promote yourself through fundraisers or golf tournaments. This is a great way to get your name out there and establish a reputation for your generosity.

1.2 Realtor gift certificate consultations

Most realtors will agree to purchase your one-hour gift certificate for a one-hour consultation with their client. They can buy this from you and insert your hard copy gift certificate in their marketing materials. The home sellers may very well be looking at several realtors before they decide whom they will choose so this becomes a great marketing tool for the realtor.

After you meet with the realtor's client for the consultation, if you want to continue with the client, you will already have established a rapport with him or her and he or she is most likely to want to continue with your other services. If there was no rapport established, you might want to give that feedback to your realtor as well.

1.3 In-depth home staging consultation

When you are talking with the seller or realtor about doing a consultation for him or her, make sure everyone agrees whether or not this will be a quick-look consultation or a more in-depth consultation that will provide the seller with recommendations. When you are doing a more in-depth consultation, it can take anywhere from two to three hours depending on the square footage of the property.

One of the areas to focus on during the in-depth consultation is *to build trust*. After all, you are dealing with most homeowners' largest asset — their house. Building great relationships means that happy clients will also give you great referrals!

Selling a home is an emotional experience for most people on some level. Sellers who are detached emotionally are typically flipping a property they do not live in and think only in terms of the Return on Investment (ROI). Other sellers might be experiencing some of the following emotions and circumstances:

- Happy to be selling
- Overwhelmed with the job ahead
- Still grieving the loss of a family member
- Downsizing due to health reasons
- Upsizing as their family grows
- Unable to afford the home any longer
- Excited to be starting a home office business and needs more space

Spend time in your consultation to explore and ask questions about how the client is feeling emotionally. There is no need to be a therapist but having great listening and empathic skills will help you tremendously in gaining trust with your client.

The following are some ways you can build trust and rapport during your in-depth consultation:

- Find out how long the seller has lived in his or her home. The longer the person has lived in his or her home the more work he or she will have to do and, possibly, more emotions will be involved. This can depend on the person's style of living (e.g., pack rat, minimalist, etc.).

- If the seller has done home improvements and upgrades in the last three to seven years, acknowledge that. The seller will feel good about keeping the house updated. Acknowledging the upgrades leaves the person with a positive feeling. It also means less work ahead for preparing the property for sale.

- If there is a lot to do in the home, clearly define a plan for the seller that offers a step-by-step approach with time frames and action steps. This would be a good client to offer your Recommendation Report (discussed in section **2.**) to so he or she has a plan and can stay focused. This will help the person to not feel so overwhelmed.

- Share your successes and experience. If you have professional training, show the client your certificate. Use your before and after photo portfolio to show him or her the work you have done for other property sellers.

- You're there to make the client feel better about this big job ahead of him or her, so find ways to compliment the person's home.

- Offer to be the person's "home staging coach" and his or her "go to" person for the duration of the project if this is going to be a long work-in-progress. The more check-ins you can do the better you and the client will feel toward ensuring the person is on track.

✓ Let the client know the areas that you can really make a difference in for the property presentation. Stress the fact that with you doing what you do best, the client can focus on things only he or she can do such as personal phone calls and paperwork associated with the move.

1.4 Color consultations

If a property is more than five years old, it is likely that it will need to be painted depending on the original color and the care of the exterior and interior walls during this time period. A color consultation is one of the most frequently purchased services by home sellers. Painting a home has one of the highest returns-on-investment and makes the biggest impact because it makes a home look updated.

When doing a color consultation here are a few key points to keep in mind when selecting paint colors:

✓ Select paint in neutral colors and use brighter, trendier colors in your accent pieces such as cushions, vases, drapes, florals, etc.

✓ If the main floor is an open concept style, use only one paint color throughout the entire floor.

✓ Keep to three colors in total throughout the house — all in neutrals so that no color is too dark or too light.

✓ Make your color selection on the flooring that is staying and make sure both the undertone in the flooring and the paint color match.

If you are not competent in doing or qualified to do a color consultation, think about taking some courses or contract with someone who is an expert in doing them. You can also go to PresStaging.com and look under "Resources"; in the archives you will find the article: "Best Color to Paint a Home for Resale."

I recommend that you have at least three paint companies as part of your strategic alliances. In busy times, such as summer, many paint companies are fully booked and will do the work for their existing clients or a stager who recommends their services often.

2. Recommendations and Reports

If clients have a lot of work to do to get their homes ready for selling, it is a good idea to promote your services by providing them with recommendations or a more formal recommendation report. Either one will get them focused on what they need to do, and offer them a road map to make their preparation for selling their homes more manageable. The Recommendation Report (see Form 3) and the Detailed Recommendation Report (see Form 4) allow you to prioritize the workload for you and the seller, and when completed give both of you an overview of the work ahead.

There are a few options home stagers can offer when making recommendations:

✓ Have the home seller take his or her own notes with the recommendation form you have provided. Tell the client what he or she needs to do so he or she can record the information on the form. (If the home is vacant, this won't be necessary because there won't be clutter or other items for the home seller to remove or pack.)

✓ Make your own notes with all of the recommendations and give that to the seller once you have completed it at the end of the consultation.

✓ Make your own notes with recommendations and later provide a typed formal Recommendation Report to the seller.

2.1 Client records recommendations

Many home sellers who are budget conscious and able to understand all the recommendations you are going to make for them will want to take notes themselves rather than pay you for your typed, formal Recommendation Report. In either case the recommendation form will work best for them.

One of the best ways to use the recommendation form is to start in the key rooms or areas. You may also make the decision to start in one room or area that is going to need the most work to prepare it for selling. Once the homeowner is clear on what needs to be done, move on to a new room or area. When you have completed the recommendation form it is a good idea to highlight or put an asterisk next to the priority items so that the home seller has a starting place. For example, if home improvements such as flooring, painting, or new window treatments are needed, it would be wise to recommend the client get started on these first since these will take longer and be a major expense.

If the seller is close to his or her actual selling time, another good idea is to put colored stickers indicating what needs to be left or removed. For example, you might try this color-coded system:

- ✔ Red: Throw out or recycle — whatever the case, the item must be removed

- ✔ Blue: Item goes to a storage locker

- ✔ Yellow: Goes to a relative

- ✔ Pink: Goes to a thrift store

- ✔ Green: Item stays

It is highly recommended that you also take your own notes to refer back to. Often sellers will start the process and get overwhelmed and may ask for your help in the end. This way you are aware from the start of what needs to be done to the property.

2.2 Your recorded recommendations

Your recorded recommendations are a quick and easy way to present recommendations to the home seller. You, with or without the client, can walk around the house outside and inside and complete the same Recommendation Report (Form 3) in preparation for typing up your information. Once you have typed it up you can email it or drop it off so that the client can begin the preparations you have recommended to get the house ready for market. It is your preference whether or not you have the client walk around with you when you take your notes.

Warning: Some homeowners may follow you around, take your ideas, do the home staging themselves, and decide they do not need to pay you for your typed Recommendation Report. To avoid this, be clear on what services you are providing and what the charges will be. However, if the clients are paying you by the hour and you are giving them suggestions, if they decide to go ahead and do the work themselves you need to accept this. They may feel they have paid you and you did such a great job explaining everything they need to do, that in the end they want to do it themselves. Most new stagers start off giving too much away and get resentful of that fact. You will learn how much to tell them, especially if you do want the home staging job, once they have done their homework.

As was mentioned earlier, when you have completed the recommendation form it is a good idea to highlight, prioritize by number, or put an asterisk next to the priority items so that the home seller has a starting place.

2.3 Detailed recommendation report

You will transfer your written notes into a typed format for the client after you have completed your tour of the home, inside and outside. It is a good idea to put your top five priorities at the

FORM 3
RECOMMENDATION REPORT

Date: _____ Home Seller: _____ Or Home Stager: _____

Room/Area	Remove	Replace with	Paint Color	Furniture Setup	Other

beginning of your report so the homeowner has a clear indicator of what needs to be done first, second, and so on. This may take a bit of time for the first few that you do, but as you do them more often, it will take less time.

In the Detailed Recommendation Report you might want to consider taking some before photos to include in your typed report and make specific recommendations referring to the photos in each room or area. The result is a huge benefit for the seller as he or she will know exactly what he or she needs to do by looking at your photo and recommendations.

Form 4 is an example of a Detailed Recommendation Report. On the CD you will find a blank version of this form for your use.

2.4 Open house or viewing checklist

Along with your Recommendation Report you can provide a generic Open House or Viewing Checklist (see Form 5) that just needs to be checked off before any open houses or showings. It is a good reference form for the home

seller to refer to once all the staging preparations have been made.

3. Professional Organizing and Prepack Services

For some clients, the more "things" they have the more overwhelming the whole process of preparing the home for selling can seem. One of the suggestions that you can make to your sellers is that by getting organized and prepacking they will not have so much to do once the property is actually sold.

Many clients will need the assistance of a professional organizer to help them to decide the following:

- What will they need to keep for daily living or for staging the home?
- What can be given away?
- What can be thrown out?
- What can be sold?
- What can be prepacked for the move?

FORM 4
DETAILED RECOMMENDATION REPORT

Client Information

Name: _____

Address: _____

Date of report: _____

Submitted by: _____

Priorities to Help You Sell Sooner!

1. Meet with the paint company and get a quote for the entire home. It is recommended that you get three quotes and select the one you feel best meets your needs. Paint each area as recommended. The Benjamin Moore paint colors selected can be matched at any paint store. I will have my painter follow up with you as one of my referrals.

2. Call contractor at phone number and have him come out and give you a quote for the shower unit, lights, and mirror in your daughter's room, and for the tiles in the en suite from the master bedroom.

3. Start the decluttering and depersonalizing on the main floor; then the downstairs rooms; have your children start the prepacking of their bedrooms and decide what to keep, throw out, give away, or sell.

4. Make a list of everything you need to buy. Once you have done that I will provide you with a quote for rental furnishings and you can then decide what you would like to do.

5. Use colored markers to highlight the work that everyone needs to do: You, your children, outside contractors, and the home staging company — this will make it clearer to see what needs to be done.

Room/Area	Challenge	Recommended Solutions
Outside/Exterior		
Exterior	• Christmas lights • Flowers on your front porch • Brass number sign is dirty • Backyard area • Inside front colored stick-on film decorations	• Take down lights all around house • Plant some colorful, attractive flowers in the pots out front • Buy some Brasso and clean your number sign • Set up your outdoor furniture in the backyard – clean it up as well • Replace colored stick-on panels on both sides of the door with opaque stick-on film

FORM 4 — CONTINUED

Inside Main Floor		
Entranceway	• Very unwelcoming entrance	• Buy or rent some art for the hallway • Buy a new area rug for the entrance • Paint entrance way the same color as the living room (CC-364 Shore Line)
Living Room	• Most of the existing leather furniture is acceptable • Tables are good for this room • Furniture needs some placement adjusting – put in a parallel shape facing each other • Too many small things in this room • Fireplace mantel is brass • Draperies are dated	• Remove traditional chair to the piano room if you keep the piano • Paint same color as entranceway and hallway (CC-364 Shore Line) • Remove all small personal objects from fireplace mantel • Remove all the plants on the floor and the small carpet • Move the stereo into the family room • Have the brass painted on the fireplace in a black matte finish • Leave the sheers on the windows but remove the blue valance and the rod that is holding them
Piano Room	• Bookcase and chairs do not work in this room • There is no art to add interest • The valance is too much in this room	• Remove bookcase and chairs (if you are going to rent a storage locker, put these in it) • Buy or rent some art for this room • Remove the valance and the rod • If you do remove the piano, turn this room back into a dining room and use your existing dining room table and chairs • Paint same color as entranceway and hallway (CC-364 Shore Line)
Family Room	• Furniture makes this room unbalanced • Furniture is blocking the outside doors • Room lacks warmth and comfort	• Reposition furniture to not block outside doors • Remove the love seat • This room needs art — rent or buy • Remove the valance topper • Remove all of the family photos • Paint the fireplace brass in a black matte paint • Bring the stereo in from the living room • Paint in CC-456 (Dufferin Terrace)

Kitchen	• Wrong style table and chairs for this kitchen • Clutter and appliances on counters	• Bring the table and chairs up from downstairs and use the two that are in the piano room right now • Put table in storage if you are not going to convert your piano room back to a dining room • Buy or rent some kitchen-type accessories • Buy or rent a nice centerpiece for the dining room table — a bowl of fruit or flowers
Hallway	• China cabinet is out of place	• Remove the china and the china cabinet. • If you are not going to change the piano room back into a dining room, then you need to store the china cabinet
Powder Room	• Too stark and cold • Needs paint color • Needs small art • Dated light fixtures	• Buy or rent some art • Buy or rent some new fluffy towels in white or dark beige-brown to warm up this room • Small accessory such as an orchid plant would work well in here • Paint in CC-364 (Shore Line) • Change light fixtures to the newer look of brushed nickel • Keep the three-light fixture look but update it. The Home Depot is an excellent store at which to find lighting fixtures.
Laundry Room	• Quite acceptable as it is	• Keep it clean and tidy as you have it • Paint in CC-456 (Dufferin Terrace)
Den	• This room is being used as an extra bedroom but will be featured best as a den/office	• Remove the bed and dresser from this room • Put the love seat from the family room in here • Remove all personal photos and belongings • Remove storage unit and storage shelf • Paint in CC-364 (Shore Line)

Inside Downstairs		
Media Room	• Needs new coat of paint • Room lacks a balanced and harmonious look • Too many things in this room • Keep television as the focal point	• Paint in CC-456 (Dufferin Terrace) • Remove table to upstairs kitchen • Move desk over to the left where table was • Remove the area rug in this room • Remove the stool • Remove all the books on the top shelf of the bookcases • Change the art in this room • Remove the stuffed animal collection
Downstairs Existing Bedroom	• Very cluttered • Large bed for this room • Curtain is dated	• Remove all the clutter and personal belongings • Purchase new bedding in neutral colors or use the bedding from Melody's room • Remove the chest • Remove the shelf • Buy or rent art • Remove the valance but leave the curtain • Clear off the shelving and tidy up the area where the built in is with the CDs in it
Downstairs Bathroom	• Stark room	• Continue with same paint color in here (Dufferin Terrace) • Buy new white waffle fabric shower curtain • Put in big fluffy towels and small piece of art • Lighting fixture is good in here

Inside Upstairs		
Master Bedroom	• Fireplace brass is dated • Desks detract from the intended elegance in this bedroom • Overall look is not good enough for a master bedroom • Bedding is fine	• Paint entire upstairs in CC-398 (Old Montreal) • Remove the two desks in this room • Remove the chair • Bring up the round table from the piano room • Buy or rent an attractive bouquet of flowers for the table • Buy or rent some attractive accessories for the fireplace mantel • Remove the existing art in this room • Buy or rent some new art for over the fireplace and over bed • Paint the brass fireplace in a black matte paint
Master Bedroom en suite	• Too cluttered and too many personal items on display • Tiles on outside of shower are wearing and therefore look dirty • Light fixture is brass and dated	• Remove all personal daily products • Buy or rent some large, fluffy, attractive towels to suit the intended elegance of the en suite • Purchase new five-piece light fixture in brushed nickel • Have bathroom renovator quote on repairing or replacing the outside tiles
Daughter's Room	• This room is way too crowded with the storage closet units and the two twin beds	• Remove the two freestanding closets • Remove all of the personal belongings • Remove all of the clutter on the desk and bookshelf • Remove the valance and the rod for the valance • Remove the bookshelf and the extra chair • Switch the twin beds for the bed in the downstairs den area; this bedding may be okay for downstairs • Buy or rent bedding for this room – neutral colors or green or blue
En suite	• Shower stall is in very poor condition • Lights and mirror are very dated and in bad shape • Cabinet has some marks on it	• Replace the existing shower unit • Replace the lighting fixtures and the mirror • Buy or rent nice, new towels • Buy or rent small piece of art for this bathroom

Guest Bedroom	• This is an attractive guest bedroom with a few exceptions	• Remove the desk • Buy or rent some new bedding in blues or greens; something warmer and more inviting • Buy or rent some art • Remove the valance and leave one rod • Remove the clutter on top of the dresser
Guest Bedroom en suite	• Needs a more updated look	• Buy a new shower curtain to go with the new bedding colors • Replace the existing six-round light fixture with a newer one in brushed nickel • Buy or rent some new towels to go with the new shower curtain and bedding

Required Follow up

[　] Let me know when you have reviewed the Detailed Recommendation Report and we will come by to review and determine the next steps.

[　] If you want to go shopping to make some new purchases, we can do that with you.

[　] If you prefer to rent some of my inventory, we can provide a quote for you.

[　] If you are unable to do any of the tasks we talked about, we are available to do them with or for you.

[　] Other: _____

Thank you for allowing my company the opportunity to provide our
Detailed Recommendation Report to you.

We know this will help you get started to sell SOONER and for TOP DOLLAR!

OPEN HOUSE OR VIEWING CHECKLIST

Outside of House (Consider hiring professionals if you are not able to complete these tasks yourself.)

[　] Sweep all walkways

[　] Manicure lawn

[　] Trim plants or bushes

[　] Trim trees

[　] Replace or add flowers

[　] Replace mailbox

[　] Pull weeds

[　] Replace or repair flower boxes

[　] Replace broken sprinklers

[　] Clean yard of debris, odds and ends, etc.

[　] Clean decks/patio

[　] Repair any roof shingles or tiles

[　] Touch up paint where needed

[　] Paint trim _____

[　] Paint front door _____

[　] Replace front door

[　] New door handle

[　] Remove wind chimes and any lawn decorations

[　] Power wash (recommended)

[　] Repairs: _____

[　] Other: _____

Pools and hot tubs:

[　] Clean hot tub and keep hot tub cover clear from water

[　] Remove hot tub

[　] Repairs: _____

Inside of House (Consider hiring professionals if you are not able to complete these tasks yourself.)

Kitchen:

Moving is a great time to purge. Anything that you have not used in six months, consider throwing away, selling at a garage sale, or giving to charity.

[　] Go through all cabinets and drawers and pack anything that you do not use on a regular basis (e.g., holiday items, platters, baking pans, dishes, glasses).

[　] Pack up toasters, coffee makers, coffee grinders, utensil holders, etc. (If you need any of these items, put them in the cabinets and take out only when you need them, then put them back when you are done.)

[　] Organize cabinets and drawers to look neat, clean, and sparse.

[　] Clean counters of all papers and unnecessary items.

[　] Clean the stove, replace burners (if needed), and replace drip bowls (if needed).

[　] Clean the inside of the refrigerator; get rid of old items, clean walls, doors, drawers, freezer, and put a fresh box of baking soda to absorb odors in the fridge.

[　] Clean the outside of the refrigerator; remove items from the top of the refrigerator. Remove: magnets, notes, photos, children's paintings, etc.

[　] Clean sink and rim around sink. If the drain for the sink has odors, you can use lemon juice and baking soda to remove the smell. Pour the baking soda in the drain then poor one cup of lemon juice and let sit for an hour then run the hot water.

[　] Repairs: _____

[　] Paint color: _____

[　] Other: _____

Bathrooms:

[　] Clean counter tops, sinks, tub, shower, toilets, etc.

[　] Remove shampoo bottles, razors, and other personal items from the tub or shower area. Store them under the counter. Use attractive baskets if needed.

[　] Clean under the cabinets, toss excess, and organize to look orderly.

[　] Store hair dryers, curling irons, brushes, etc., in baskets under the counter.

[　] Clean floors, floor boards, and walls.

[　] Use decorative bath towel sets (hanging) and hand towels on the counter. Use an older set of towels for personal use while the house is on the market. Put away when done.

[　] When done using the shower or tub, wipe it clean.

[　] If you have shower doors, keep them clean and dry.

[　] Remove all floor mats.

[   ] Paint color: _____

[   ] Other: _____

Living Room:

[   ] Clean floors

[   ] Clean windows

[   ] Clean walls

[   ] Entertainment center: Pack CDs, movies, and DVDs.

[   ] Clear off coffee and end tables of any excess items, tissue, remotes, etc.

[   ] Pack all unnecessary items

[   ] Repairs: _____

[   ] Paint color: _____

[   ] Other: _____

Fireplaces:

[   ] Empty and clean: Use BBQ or fireplace black matte spray paint on old brass frames and paint the inside of the fireplace if necessary.

[   ] Fireplaces are considered one of the "big emotional sellers" in most homes so make sure it looks good. Add something attractive over the fireplace with a few accessories so that the eye is immediately drawn to this focal point.

Bedrooms:

[   ] Clean or replace carpets

[   ] Clean windows and walls

[   ] Pack CDs, movies, and DVDs

[   ] Remove TV

[   ] Pack all family photos and collectibles

[   ] Clear clutter from nightstands

[   ] Pack all unnecessary items

[   ] Keep beds made: Use new bedding and "hotel look" bedding in the master bedroom

[   ] Repairs: _____

[   ] Paint color: _____

[   ] Other: _____

In the staging industry the word *prepack* gets clients thinking about their future home and not dwelling on the moving. With prepacking they will decide what they want to go with them into their new home. This can also be a great benefit to stagers if the seller has some home decor items that you really do not want to use for the staging! You will tactfully suggest they prepack the item so it stays in perfect condition for the new home. For example, a collection that is dear to them may not enhance the look of the home for selling.

Most professional organizers will give their client an overall plan of what needs to be done and then work room-by-room or area-by-area with them for a few hours a day. The homeowner is typically given homework to carry on with, organizing and prepacking a little bit each day to achieve the goal.

Here are some suggestions to help your client get organized:

- Encourage your client to make a list in each room of what they *need* to have in order to live comfortably from the time the property is on the market to the time the home sells.

- From this starting-point list, the client can then decide what to do with all the rest of the things he or she does not need at this time.

- You can also advise the client on what you would like left in the room so that you can use it for the actual staging of the home. Tagging items with colored sticky dots or notes makes it easier for the client to know what should stay and what should go.

- From all the other items that are not being prepacked the seller can decide what he or she wants to do with those items.

- If the client needs to get rid of things, you can provide your list of where he or she can take the unwanted items (e.g., auction houses, junk removal companies, charitable organizations, ReStores, Habitat for Humanity, and recycling companies). Some sellers might be inclined to hold a garage sale.

- Many sellers will need to get a storage locker for things you do not want to use for the staging, and that they want to keep. Since they will need the services of a moving company they can also get boxes, packing tape, and labels to make the job easier.

- If there is a PODS company in the area, this company's services might be the right fit for your client so you can recommend this to them as an option for a storage container. PODS will bring the right size container to the client and park it at street level so they can just walk in with their storage items. PODS can be stored on- or off-site.

- Some older clients who may be downsizing or moving into care facilities have found it helpful to have a family gathering where family members decide on the things they would like to have.

I recommend that clients not use their spare bedroom or garage for storing their items. This translates into "not enough storage space" to the potential home buyer, which is not a good thing since people are always looking for lots of storage space!

3.1 Downsizing recommendations

Some of your clients will be at a point in their lives where they are ready to leave their long-time home and downsize. Often these clients will want your advice on what they should take to their new home since they realize they won't be able to take everything with them. Many will have floor plans or may ask you to go to their new property to see what you think will fit and work best in the new space. This can be an advantage for you as you may not want some of the pieces for staging purposes that they do want to keep.

While some home stagers are certified interior decorators, many have a natural decorating talent and are capable of delivering some of the services that an interior decorator would provide. Some other services that you can offer the downsizing client include:

- ✓ Selecting new and smaller furniture and home decor items for the new home.

- ✓ Selecting products such as tiles, flooring, and window treatments.

- ✓ Looking at furniture, art, and accessory placement in the new home.

- ✓ Color selection if the new home needs repainting.

- ✓ Move-in services such as setting up the client's new home the way he or she wants it for living and not for selling.

4. Sourcing for Rental Furnishings

Sourcing is a term used in the home staging industry originating from when a stager needed to find sources, that is, products from wholesale or retail stores for vacant home staging. Since staging has become more popular, rental furnishing stores that supply inventory to stagers are springing up in most major cities. Stagers will spend a fair amount of time sourcing what products they need from a rental furnishing store depending on the size of the property they are staging.

When stagers do not have rental furnishing companies in their area, many will have their own smaller inventory to enhance the look of the homes they are staging. Even if you are sourcing from your own inventory you will charge for the service of selecting what will work best with each property.

Before you begin the project know what your client's budget is so you are not overspending on rentals the client cannot afford at this time.

4.1 Sourcing from rental furnishing companies

In the beginning sourcing for a project can take longer than you think so give yourself extra time for your first few times of doing it. The most efficient way to do the sourcing is to follow these steps:

- ✓ Take photos of all the rooms/areas and take this with you to the store. If you get your photos printed with a matte finish, you can write or draw on them if you want to decide where your selections will work best.

- ✓ Make a list of the inventory that you need for *each* room whether you are doing the entire vacant home or only some of it. You can use the Inventory List (Form 6) provided or make a list of your own by using the Inventory List provided on the CD.

Note that there is a column for describing the inventory by adding a SKU (Stock-Keeping Unit). Some home stagers add a SKU to their products in order to keep track of their inventory.

Once you have made your first list of what you need for each room or area, you will make another list of the *products* you need for each room. This allows you to cross-check your products. It also allows for quicker selection when you are in the store or in your storage locker. Most rental furniture companies will have all the sofas, chairs, art, florals, and accessories together to make it less time consuming when picking what you need. This way you can work in one area of the store or your storage locker and then move to another area to save time. You can make a list or use the Inventory Cross-Check List (Form 7) provided on the CD.

It is critical to the outcome of your staging job that you decide on the color scheme for the home. It is often easiest to pick out one of your main pieces of art with at least three colors in it and work with this throughout the home.

Most store employees will be happy to work with you to find the perfect fit for your client's staging style and budget. Having your list of what you need helps you select your products more easily. Once you have made your selection the store will provide you with a quote that you can review with your client. It may happen in the beginning that your quote comes in too high for the client's budget. You can revisit your selections and eliminate or change a few of your pieces.

Some stagers mark up the inventory they are renting and pay the rental furnishing company directly. If you do this, it may mean you are responsible for all the inventory coming back in the same condition it went out. This arrangement is fine if it is a vacant home, but can be challenging if someone is living in the home and using the rentals on a daily basis. Many stagers have the client deal directly with the rental furnishing company so that they are not responsible should anything go missing or be damaged. Know what the terms and conditions are with any rental furnishing company and decide which route is best for you.

4.1a Terms and conditions for rental furnishing companies

Every rental furnishing company will offer their own terms and conditions. When you have to consider using a rental furnishing company for all or partial staging keep in mind the following:

- First month's rental fees are usually for a one-month time period.

- Rentals after the first month might be pro-rated or charged on a weekly basis, or for the entire month regardless of the length of time the rentals were actually used.

- The inventory rental payment is automatically put through on the due date of the second month without notification to the home seller (if it is on the person's credit card or he or she has used a postdated check).

- Rental fees usually go down after the third month but some may decrease sooner than this.

- Check to find out when deliveries can be made with the rental furnishing company. If you are moving rentals into a condominium, find out what times the elevator is free for the move.

- When the rentals are delivered to you they are usually in bins that may or may not be marked by room or area. You will need to find a place for the rental bins once you have unloaded everything. At times you may need to take them home with you as there may not be space in the seller's home.

- You will be responsible for packing up the rentals, so you will need to keep in touch with the seller to find out when the property has sold so you can pick up the inventory.

FORM 6
INVENTORY LIST

Main Floor				
Room	**Inventory**	**Description /SKU**	**Quantity**	**Cost**
Living Room	Sofa Chairs Love seat Art Coffee table Side tables Lamps Accessories Florals Area rug			
Family Room	Sofa Love seat Chairs Art Coffee table Accessories			
Dining Room	Dining table Chairs Art Accessories			
Kitchen	Accessories Small bistro table Chairs Plant			
Hallway	Table Art Accessories			
Office	Desk Art Plant or florals			
Powder Room	Art Accessory Towels			

Upstairs				
Master Bedroom	Blow-up bed: Queen Headboard: Queen Bedding: King Bedskirt Shams Throw Accessories Floral or large tree Chair Bedside tables			
En suite Bathroom	Art Towels Florals Accessories			
	Total			

✓ The person who signs the rental agreement is responsible for the inventory if the items are damaged, lost, or stolen. The typical replacement price is the retail price to repurchase the goods.

✓ Most homeowners have homeowners' insurance, so if they are living in the home, they would be responsible for the inventory.

4.2 Sourcing from your own inventory

Many home stagers start out buying small inventory items such as bedding, accessories, art, florals, lamps, and area rugs. These are things they can easily move in and out of their car.

If you do source from your own inventory, you can charge for the sourcing and rentals of the inventory. You may decide to purchase your own large inventory such as sofas, chairs, dining tables, beds, etc. If you do, you will be investing a large amount of money, perhaps up to $50,000, to buy enough furnishings for two or three homes. You will also need to allow for your own storage fees unless you have space in your garage or can get some for free.

Many stagers charge a "small accessory package" price of between $150 and $300 depending on what they are renting. In major cities the standard for determining the inventory rental fee is 25 percent of the retail cost rented on a per-month basis. If you are a professional home stager with a business number, you can buy furnishings wholesale by setting up an account with wholesale suppliers. If you do this, you would most likely be purchasing products at 50 percent of the retail price. You can decide what works best for you and your market.

INVENTORY CROSS-CHECK LIST

Main Floor	
Accessories	
LR – Coffee table	
LR – Console table	
Hall	
DR – Table	
BN – Bistro table	
Kitch – Counter	
Office – Desk	
Area Rugs	
LR	
Art	
LR – Over fireplace Over console	
DR – On west wall	
Hall	
Office	
Breakfast nook	
Powder room	
Floral/Plants	
LR – Vase twigs	
Powder room on commode	
Office corner vase/plant	
BN – Plant	
Furniture	
LR – Sofa Love seat	
DR – Table 4 Chairs	
Office – Desk Chair	
BN – v2 Chairs	

FORM 7 — CONTINUED

Lamps	
LR – Floor	
Other Tables	
LR – Coffee	
BN – Bistro	
Hall – Console small	
Upstairs – Master Bedroom	
Accessories	
On table by chair On bed Throw for chair En suite	
Art	
Above chair En suite	
Bed	
Coverlet/Duvet Pillows Shams Headboard	
Furniture	
Blow-up bed Chair Bedside tables	
Lamps	
For bedside tables Floor for chair	

If you do decide to start building your inventory, you will need to track it. The Real Estate Staging Association (RESA) has inventory software that you can purchase. Just go to RESA's website and search under "Resources for Stagers."

5. Shopping

I know some of you will find this a stretch — to go shopping and get paid for it! Alas there are some things you need to do to help your clients and this can be one of them! Many clients will ask you to shop for them for home decor purchases or they will want you to come with them while they shop for staging props that they will purchase. You can decide what works best for you and the clients.

If you are going shopping for the clients, it is advisable to get a retainer from them. Determine what you think their purchases will cost and request the amount from them. You can decide to charge merchandise on your credit card but know that if anything does need to be returned that you will have to do it. Getting a check or cash from them is a good way to deal it it, and ensure you provide them with receipts in case they want to return anything. If you are doing the returning, you can charge for this service as well. Either way, make a list of what you need to purchase so you can do the shopping as quickly as possible. You might want to make a list to make the shopping go quickly and efficiently.

You can choose to shop in either retail or wholesale stores. If you want to do wholesale shopping, you will need proof you're shopping for your business. You may be required to purchase a large volume of product before you get a discount; just ask what the store policy is. In most retail stores if you say you are buying for your business you may get 10 to 20 percent off right then and there, or you may need to apply to get a store card for future discount purchases.

HomeSense has become a favorite for home stagers across North America. Their prices are very affordable and the products are trendy enough for staging in any city. It is recommended that you find the best stores in your area and go there frequently so you know what products are available. Stores such as HomeSense offer one-stop shopping and can be great for making good use of your time, money, and energy.

IKEA is another one-stop shopping store with affordable prices and trendy products. If you are a savvy shopper you will find great deals in many stores including Walmart and The Home Depot in both the US and Canada; Kmart and Lowe's in the US; and RONA and Canadian Tire in Canada.

6. Hands-on Staging or Installation

Hands-on staging or installation is the only service offering in which you will need to have someone working with you. All the other services you can do easily on your own, unless you want to bring someone with you for a second opinion. Some stagers try to do hands-on staging or installations by themselves but it is not recommended. It is a hard job by yourself and over time you will be putting extra stress and strain on your body. In some cases, on very large jobs you will need a team of stagers.

If you are having rental inventory delivered by a rental furnishing company, typically the movers are incredibly helpful and will put the heavy furniture where you want it. This is helpful when dealing with heavy sofas and chairs if you need to go up or down stairs.

In the beginning you may find it hard to determine how long it will take you to stage a home. The amount of "homework" or staging preparation the client has done before will help you assess how long the actual hands-on work will take. Many smaller jobs, and particularly condominiums, can easily be staged in one day. If you're doing a larger home, have a plan so you know which rooms need to be done first.

If the client is doing small or large renovations, make sure you know when those will be completed. Some staging jobs get pushed back because the renovations have not been completed on time. Always confirm with your clients the actual days you will be in the home to keep things running smoothly.

The rooms that you are going to stage are generally determined at your consultation and, therefore, before you arrive. If you are working for a realtor, you may not have seen the client's home and you may be asked to work on it right away.

After you have finished, it is a good idea to have your clients take photos of what you want the home to look like for the showings, whether private or public open houses. You can also offer to take photos and email them to your clients. Many sellers find this very helpful especially if they have children and busy lives; they can forget how it looked when you staged it!

7. MLS and Internet Photos

Many stagers offer to provide the MLS (Multiple Listing Service) photos after they have finished the hands-on staging. This is when the property looks its best. Also there are many realtors who have their own team of photographers and videographers.

One of the most disappointing situations with Internet listings is when there are already photos or videos up on the posting, and then you come in to do the staging, and they do not change the photos or video. It happens, so follow up with the home seller or realtor to ensure the latest and greatest photos are up to really show the property at its best.

8. Open-House Ready Check-in

The open-house ready check-in is a good service to offer your clients. If you have provided the hands-on staging a while ago, it is a nice touch to come in and do a little bit of "fluffing" for the home seller. If you have done the staging more recently, you could drop by with some flowers for the clients.

It is also the perfect opportunity to leave your business cards and a postcard, rack card, or flyer, with your client's or realtor's permission. Perhaps a coupon with $100 off or a free consultation would work too!

9. Pack up — Destaging

You will only be concerned with offering the pack-up service if you rented any inventory — your inventory or some from a rental furnishing store. Once the property has sold you will need to return and pack up everything. In staging this is called "destaging" and only applies when you have rentals.

If any of the rentals have been damaged, lost, or stolen, you will need to talk with the homeowner about this. If the client has signed an insurance agreement with a rental furnishing company, the client will need to deal with the rental company directly for any charges. If you have rented the furnishings to the client, you need to settle this with him or her.

Ultimately you are responsible for keeping in touch with the house seller to find out when the house has been sold. Once it is sold, if you have rented furniture, it is your responsibility to make arrangements for the rental inventory pick up from the property. You need to pack up the items carefully and return the items in the bins and boxes that were provided by the rental furnishing company.

Bring in all your inventory forms so that you can check off every item as you pack it. This applies to checking your inventory returns or those going back to rental furnishing companies.

10. Other Related Home Staging Services

Depending on your previous experience before you became a home stager you may have other skill sets that you can offer your clients. Many home stagers have taken other courses that are industry related so they can offer full color consultations, interior decorating, or interior design skills. If you have done your own home improvements or renovations, you may be knowledgeable in these areas. That knowledge will add to your tool kit and create the opportunity for you to offer more services than the average stager.

Only offer to do work that you have the qualifications for (proper skills and experience). If you do not have the skill sets but would still like to work with the clients, this would be the perfect time to refer one of your alliances to do that work. Clients love it when you find solutions to their problems. (See Chapter 14 for more information about strategic alliances.)

10.1 Interior decorating or interior design

If you have a diploma or certificate in interior decorating, you could offer such services as color consultations, fabric recommendations for reupholstering, furniture buying, and window treatments. Many stagers do not have credentials in these areas and are self-taught. If you feel you can confidently do this work, add it to your service line.

If you have a designation as an interior designer, your skill set will also include more services and, in particular, renovations. Your expertise would allow you to offer kitchen and bathroom ideas and plans that interior decorators would not be qualified to offer.

10.2 Project management

Some home stagers have the skills and experience necessary to manage projects such as preparing a property for selling that is undergoing home improvements or renovations. This is very time consuming and it is an important task to keep all the projects within budget and on time. It might involve but not be limited to coordinating contractors, painters, flooring companies, design stores, plumbers, and electricians.

If you do have this experience, you would be well advised to not take on this aspect of home staging. Most project managers provide an overall cost for the project management rather than hourly pricing.

10.3 Move-ins

Most home stagers should be able to provide a move-in service to their clients. The main difference between the staging and the move-in is that for move-in, you want to set up the home so that it is very personal and full of the clients' treasures and collections. The move-in is a fantastic service to offer since most clients have established a rapport with you; they trust you. They may be so exhausted after the preparing and sale of their home that they are happy to have you set up their new home.

A move-in is often done a few days or weeks after the clients have moved. Homeowners tend to get their personal rooms such as bedrooms and bathrooms set up right away and may not have the time to focus on the common areas such as living, family, and dining rooms.

After reading this chapter, complete Exercise 17 to help you decide what services you are comfortable offering clients right now. You can also use the exercise to rate your skills and services. It is only by *doing* this, that you can increase your confidence level of service delivery. Create your goals based on the rating that you would like to give yourself in the future.

HOME STAGING SERVICES YOU WILL OFFER

Home Staging Services	My Rating Now (10 is highest)	My Rating in Three Months

11
Pricing Guidelines

This is perhaps the most challenging chapter to write since pricing your business services is mostly dependent on what your clients are willing to pay in your area for home staging services. Your clients will be looking for *fair market value* of your services and in some towns and cities this will already be established; in others, you may be setting the pricing.

Most new home stagers tend to charge an hourly rate. This can help you in the beginning to understand exactly how much *value* you are giving your clients for that hourly rate. Many times after a full day of hands-on home staging you may wish you had charged 20 times what you did because now you understand how much goes into the physical aspect of setting up a home for selling!

As you grow your business I recommend that you start by offering staging packages. The best way is to offer your clients the choice of three packages. You can start with a basic

package, add more value to the second one, and make your third package the most expensive with the most value-added services.

Since home staging is not governed by a regulating body in North America, much of the pricing for services and even rental inventory has been established by the pioneers in the industry. The information in this chapter is based on already established pricing which I have sourced from viewing home stagers' websites and talking with other home stagers. This information comes from many home staging organizations such as Professional Real Estate Stagers (PRES), Real Estate Staging Association (RESA), Canadian ReDesigners Association (CRDA), Canadian Staging Professionals (CSP), Accredited Staging Professionals (ASP), and Interior Redesign Industry Specialists (IRIS). It is also from some of the information I have gathered while teaching home staging for over half a decade.

1. Hourly Pricing

As was discussed in Chapter 10, many of the services that you offer can be billed on an hourly basis. You can also provide all of these services by yourself so you do not need to pay someone else to assist you. These could include:

- ✓ Consultations
- ✓ Color consultations
- ✓ Organizing and prepacking
- ✓ Sourcing
- ✓ Shopping
- ✓ MLS or Internet photos

Some stagers think they should charge less for sourcing or shopping, yet the client is paying for your expertise so it is not recommended that you charge any less for these services.

You can charge whatever your market will bear; however, we want to keep the home staging industry at a professional level, and charging lower than recommended prices devalues home staging services for all home stagers. Professional home stagers who have taken courses and attended workshops in related subjects have invested time, money, and energy into becoming the best that they can be. It is important to value your investment in yourself. Based on North American home staging research these are the typical prices professional home stagers are charging:

- ✓ Average professional home staging hourly rate: minimum $75 per hour
- ✓ Metropolitan areas home staging hourly rate: $150 per hour
- ✓ Average consultation time: Two to three hours

You can charge much higher than the recommended starting hourly rate at any time. I suggest this as a starting point for you. If you do charge less, eventually you will get the reputation for being the lowest and may miss out on the higher paying and more professional home staging jobs because of it.

Know that in the beginning you may feel you are undercharging or feel uncertain about what you should charge. In time, and with more experience, you will know the value of your services and how long it takes to provide the services you are quoting. You are going to make mistakes, which is a good thing since you will be learning from them!

2. Detailed Recommendation Report Pricing

If you are going to include a Detailed Recommendation Report, you might want to consider basing your pricing on the square footage of the home. For example, your pricing for a Detailed Recommendation Report based on square footage might look like this:

- ✓ Properties (most likely condominiums) from 650 to 1,500 square feet: $250
- ✓ Properties from 1,500 to 2,500 square feet: $350
- ✓ Properties from 2,500 to 3,500: $450
- ✓ Properties from 3,500 and up: $550

Some home sellers are going to need more guidance so you will need to create a more formal report for them. They may also have a huge amount of clutter to get rid of, and organizing and prepacking to do. Another factor to consider when you are doing your pricing is how much of the property is actually going to be staged. It is very important to let clients know you can do as little or as much of the actual work that you have recommended to them, either in the consultation or in the detailed report. Many sellers end up doing some of the work, and then have you come back in to do what they cannot do.

Once you have typed this report you will need to meet with the sellers and do a thorough presentation with them.

3. Proposal or Bid Pricing

When staging was first introduced in the 1980s in the United States the only people to ask for a proposal or a bid package were realtors. This has changed in today's marketplace where you will now find that sellers are asking for proposals or bids to determine which home staging company they want to hire.

Many home sellers in metropolitan areas are more knowledgeable about home staging. They want to get the best value for their money so they may request bids or proposals from at least three home staging companies. It is important when your seller is making a comparison between your company and another company that they are comparing apples to apples and not apples to oranges. This is why it is important in your proposal or bid to be specific about some of the differences between your company and another home staging company. This is also called your "Unique Selling Proposition" or "Unique Selling Point" (USP). Present yourself and your written proposal in the most professional way possible. Sellers do not always look for the lowest bid and go with that. If they are discerning, they will also look at the *value* of what you are offering them.

When you are providing a bid, you are not going to be quoting hourly rates, rather you will be quoting by the project. You will also want to calculate into your quote what you are paying your assistants for staging and destaging the project. If you plan on having some assistance in anything other than these two

areas, remember to calculate that in as well. For example, if you prefer to take another stager with you to do the sourcing for a large property, you will want to calculate that into your bid as well.

If you are going to provide a bid, it is mandatory that you meet with the clients and conduct an in-depth overview of the staging work that needs to be done. During this time you will be building rapport with the clients; you will be listening to what their needs are; and asking questions about budget, time frames, and finding out who else is providing a bid, and when the decision will be made. You will want to take a lot of photographs to be able to reflect on when writing your proposal. If inventory is required, photos are mandatory for your selection of furnishings and ultimately to the success of this project.

While you are taking your tour of the home, inside and outside, make notes for yourself and do not give too much away! The sellers may be asking you questions such as "What color should I paint this room?" or "Do I need to remove my sewing machine from the living room?" or "Are there too many dolls in my china cabinet?" If they really want answers to all of these questions, this now becomes a consultation, which you will need to let them know there is a charge for. Otherwise, try responding this way: "These are great questions. I am putting my proposal together taking all of these into consideration." There is an expectation that if you are providing a bid that there will be no charge for this so, again, don't give too much away!

Note: If you do not win the bid, make sure you find out who did and why. The answers will help you to prepare for future estimates and bids as you grow your business.

3.1 Bid for services only

You may be asked to do a home staging estimate or submit a bid for your services only. Put this together in a nice folder along with two of your business cards and a postcard or rack card, if you have one. Remember it's all about creating a fantastic first impression through you and your marketing materials. Consider what other materials you could include that would impress your client. Do it up professionally.

These services could include:

- ✓ Consultation
- ✓ Color consultation
- ✓ Recommendation Report
- ✓ Shopping
- ✓ Hands-on staging

There are a few options that you can take when you put your quote together for just services. As mentioned previously, it is best to put a total sum for all the services and not to quote hourly rates for each.

You also need to keep accurate records of the time that you spend or expect to spend on each service item.

3.2 Services with rentals

Oftentimes you will be asked to provide a quote for your services along with rental furnishing costs. If a property is vacant, you will want to supply rentals to furnish it. If a property needs only a few rentals, you can either supply these or source them from a rental furnishing company.

It is really important to know if you are bidding against a staging company that supplies all of its own rental furnishings. The reason for this is that if another staging company does have its own large inventory (e.g., sofas, chairs, beds, etc.), they can afford to play with their rates more than you can if you are renting big furniture items from a furniture rental store.

Most home stagers have smaller inventory items such as bedding, cushions, pillows, towels, florals, plants, vases, art, and miscellaneous accessories so they can make some extra money using these for staging. Some clients may want to buy a home stager's rentals so be prepared for this! One of the best ways to offer your home staging inventory is to call it an "Inventory Package" without being too specific about what it contains for the quote. You may want to add certain inventory, but by the time the bid comes around that particular inventory may already be rented. This can also happen with rental furnishing companies.

Most rental furnishing companies give home stagers a discount. The discount can be for the first month and may be reduced in the subsequent month. This discount is entirely up to the rental furnishing company. If you use one company more than another, it would be advisable to request you get more of a discount than the stager who only occasionally sources from that rental furnishing company.

You may have some of your own smaller inventory and only need to rent larger items from a rental furnishing company. If you rent directly from a rental furnishing company, you can mark up the rentals. However, if you are marking up the rentals, you will need to supply an invoice directly to your client for this rather than having the rental furnishing store do that.

4. Exclusive Realtor-Arrangement Pricing

You may find that you have one or possibly two realtors whom you work with who give you 90 to 95 percent of your business. If this is the case, you would be wise to offer those realtors

FORM 8
PROPOSAL ESTIMATE FOR SERVICES ONLY

Home Staging Proposal Estimate for Services Only

for

(Insert client's name)
(Insert client's address)

Submitted By: *(Insert your name)*
(Insert your company's name)

*(**Note:** The above section will be the title page to the proposal and put as the first page to the report with no other information on it.)*

Date:

Client Name:
Client Address:
City, State or Province, Zip Code or Postal Code:

RE: Home Staging Quote

Dear *(Insert client's first name)*,

Thank you for this opportunity to provide a quote for your home to be staged to sell at the end of month.

Our goal is to make the selling of your house a pleasant experience for you. By taking away the stress and physical labor required to get your property prepared, you can focus on the things you need to do. Our expertise is creating properties that set themselves apart from others on the market. Our experience has proven time and again that the homes we stage sell sooner and for more money than similar homes on the market that were not staged.

You have beautiful furnishings that will really make a fantastic first impression for prospective buyers looking online and in person. With the few new items we will need to shop for, your home will be sure to impress — first time, every time!

Feel free to contact me at any time with questions or concerns you may have.

Sincerely,

(Insert your name)
(Insert your title, for example, president)
(Insert your company's name)

Recent Home Staging Projects

On this page you will insert before and after photos (at least two) of previous work you have done.

Client Testimonials

"We never could have managed on our own. *(Name of company)* did such an amazing job with every single room in our home. You transformed two rooms we weren't even using into a great looking den and a bedroom! Our living room and family room are gorgeous. We sold virtually at the open house and had multiple offers. Selling so quickly has allowed us to buy the home of our dreams! What an amazing experience to hire professionals who know what they are doing!"

(Client's first name only and city or town)

"Without her help we would have been divorced! This was a much bigger job than we ever anticipated. Can't thank you enough for saving our marriage *and* selling our house! As you know I was concerned about the paint colors you picked because they seemed so boring to me. Wow! Was I ever wrong. They look fantastic and every single room just flows and flows. Well done!"

(Client's first name only and city or town)

(The final page of the proposal will include the home staging estimate.)

Home Staging Estimate

Client Information
Submitted to: _____
Date: _____

Home Staging Services

Consultation:	$250.00
Typed Recommendation Report:	$350.00
Color Consultation:	$200.00
Shopping Services:	$300.00
Home Staging:	$1,250.00
Open House Check In:	Complimentary (no charge)
Total Estimate:	$2,350.00 plus applicable taxes

FORM 8 — CONTINUED

This is an estimated amount of time and may differ when the work is finally completed. This estimate has been provided based on the information gathered during our first consultation meeting. We always endeavor to stay on budget and on time.

Acknowledgement

Accepted by: _____
Dated: _____

50% Deposit Required: $1,175.00 plus applicable taxes

Paid by: [   ] Cash   [   ] Check   [   ] Visa   [   ] MasterCard   [   ] Other

Balance owing due on completion of work: $1,175.00 plus applicable taxes

exclusive pricing when they use your home staging services. For example, if your hourly rate is typically $150, you could reduce it to $125. You could reduce your pricing for all of your other services in a similar manner.

Consider doing marketing events such as trade shows and talks together with the realtor. You could create some marketing materials with both of your companies on them as well as have your separate materials. This way both you and the realtor can benefit from this arrangement and get twice the exposure by working closely together.

Home Staging Proposal Estimate with Rental Inventory

for

(Insert client's name)
(Insert client's address)

Submitted By: *(Insert your name)*
(Insert your company's name)

*(**Note:** The above section will be the title page to the proposal and put as the first page to the report with no other information on it.)*

Date:

Client Name:
Client Address:
City, State or Province, Zip Code or Postal Code:

RE: Home Staging Estimate with Rental Inventory

Dear *(Insert client's first name),*

Thank you for this opportunity to provide a quote for your home to be staged to sell at the end of month.

Our goal is to make the selling of your house a pleasant experience for you. By taking away the stress and physical labor required to get your property prepared, you can focus on the things you need to do. Our expertise is creating properties that set themselves apart from others on the market. Our experience has proven time and again that the homes we stage sell sooner and for more money than a similar home on the market that was not staged.

You have beautiful furnishings that will really make a fantastic first impression for prospective buyers looking online and in person. With the "Inventory Package" from *(insert your company name)* I know your home will be sure to impress — first time, every time!

Feel free to contact me at any time with questions or concerns you may have.

Sincerely,

(Insert your name)
(Insert your title, for example, president)
(Insert your company's name)

Recent Home Staging Projects with Rental Inventory

On this page you will insert before and after photos (at least two) of previous work you have done.

Client Testimonials

"We were absolutely amazed at how fantastic our home looks. We never would have thought of all the creative ways that you have put the rooms together. You were right about saying the way we live in our home is not the way we sell it. By adding your beautiful accessories you really updated the look of the home. The best news of course for us is that we have three offers now! We can breathe a sigh of relief because your company took away all the stress that had me feeling overwhelmed. Thanks again."

(Client's first name only and city or town)

"I've become a believer! With just those things you brought in such as the art, the flowers, the new bedding, and some cushions, you really made our condo a showcase. The way you positioned the furniture is not anything we would have done. Love the way the bedrooms look so much bigger — well, they are, because of all the clutter we got rid of! Love it, love it, love it!"

(Client's first name only and city or town)

(The final page of the proposal will include the home staging estimate.)

Home Staging Estimate with Inventory

Client Information

Submitted to: _____

Date: _____

Home Staging Services

Consultation:	$250.00
Color Consultation:	$200.00
Small Inventory Rental Package:	$500.00

- Master bedroom
- En suite
- Living room
- Family room
- Dining room

Home Staging:	$1,250.00
Open House Check In:	Complimentary (no charge)
Total Estimate:	$2,200.00 plus applicable taxes

Rental Inventory

(Insert your company's name) inventory is rented on a monthly basis from the date of the home staging. Payment is due for the second month on the anniversary date of the installation. If you go into a third month of inventory rentals, we will reduce that fee by 50%, and for subsequent months if needed. An itemized Inventory List along with Terms and Conditions will be provided to you upon acceptance of this home staging estimate.

This is an estimated amount of time and may differ when the work is finally completed. This estimate has been provided based on the information you provided us. We always endeavor to stay on budget and on time.

Acknowledgement

Accepted by: _____
Dated: _____

50% Deposit Required: $1,100.00 plus applicable taxes

Paid by: [   ] Cash   [   ] Check   [   ] Visa   [   ] MasterCard   [   ] Other

Balance owing due on completion of work: $1,100.00 plus applicable taxes

12
Sales Cycle for Home Staging Services

In previous chapters you learned about the marketing strategies and tools you will be using in your business; now you will be introduced to the selling skills you need to ensure the success of your business. Your marketing strategies and tools provide the avenue for *educating* and *informing* clients about what you do. Your selling skills are what will *close the sale* so that you have revenues coming in to support your marketing efforts.

For some new and even some seasoned home stagers, selling is uncomfortable and often the last thing they want to do. However, without it your business will never grow. In the beginning you will need to find clients whether they are realtors or home sellers. As your business grows the goal will be to have clients looking for you, instead of you searching for them! Clients can come through referrals from

home sellers and realtors you have worked with in the past, or third-party referrals where someone you worked with recommends you. With practice your confidence will grow and you will find it easier to close the sale.

There are generally two types of selling styles. There is the *soft sell* approach and the *hard sell* approach. Most clients you will come in contact with will prefer the soft sell approach. The soft sell approach is considered less pushy and not so aggressive — probably what you yourself prefer. The hard sell can often make the prospect feel uncomfortable and feel forced into making decisions he or she may later regret. This is often called *push* marketing and selling.

Stagers, like other professionals, follow a typical sales cycle from prospecting to closing the sale. The sales cycle can vary somewhat but generally follows a sequential pattern so it is easy to follow. You may find at times you have changed the steps in the cycle, not to worry; the end goal is to get the sale!

At this point you may be unfamiliar with some standard sales terminology. Here are a few terms you need to become familiar with:

- **Prospect:** A potential client (i.e., realtor or home seller).

- **Cold calling:** Making a call to someone you do not know.

- **Qualifying:** Asking your prospect questions to see if he or she will be a good client, finding out the urgency of putting the person's home on the market, and finding out specifically what he or she sees as his or her challenges are particularly important if the property has been on the market and is not selling.

- **Features and benefits:** Discussion of what you have to offer and the benefits.

- **Handling objections:** Responding to negative concerns.

- **Trial close:** Getting a "yes" before you finally ask for the sale.

- **Client or customer:** After the prospect has bought your services he or she becomes the client or customer.

- **Close:** You ask for the business and you either get it or you don't.

1. Typical Sales Cycle

If you are new to owning your own business and selling your services you will find this sales cycle helpful as it is very systematic and can be learned by doing. You can always practice on a few friends and start out with small sales that are not so high risk such as bidding on a $5,000 job as your first client! The following sections provide you with what a typical sales cycle looks like for home stagers.

1.1 Prospecting

Prospecting is a term used in sales to determine who has the potential to become a client or customer. Like a gold miner, you need to do your prospecting to find the "gold." Ideally, you want to turn your prospect into a client, which is gold to you. By following the steps in this typical sales cycle you will be able to do just that!

Almost anyone you talk to will be a prospect for you. Even if the people you talk to directly don't need your services themselves, they may know someone who does. If they do refer you, this is called a *third-party referral*. The good news is, realistically, your staging prospects can be found everywhere!

1.2 Qualifying

Qualifying is a term used to determine whether or not the prospect is actually going to buy your services. In staging you will have a lot of people inquiring about your services and this is when you need to find out who is really interested in buying what you have to offer.

You need to find out what is *motivating* your prospects to hire you. You need to be able to answer their question, "What's in it for me?" Some of the more common questions will focus around saving them time, money, and energy. You may hear the following questions:

- How much money will I make if I stage my home?

- How much money will I save if I listen to you?

- How much sooner can you get my property ready to sell than I can?

✓ Can you save me time because I am running out of it?

✓ Can you tell me exactly what to keep so I can start now?

One of the concerns to focus on in qualifying any client is to find out just how *urgent* their need is. Some prospects may be thinking about selling in the next year or so while others may decide they want to put their property on the market next week. Be prepared for any variety of time-frame scenarios.

Realtors as well as home sellers often do not realize what is involved with getting a home prepared for the market. If rental furnishings are involved, this can take longer than just going into the seller's home to make minor staging adjustments using only his or her furnishings. So, ask the question, "How soon do you want to put your property on the market?" From here you know how much or how little time you have to do the work, should the person hire you.

Two other questions when qualifying prospects are to find out how much the property is going to list for, and what their budget for staging is. You will find many of these key questions are part of your Client Consultation (Form 1) provided on the CD and in Chapter 10.

You may be communicating with prospects over the phone, via email, or in person. You can qualify them by simply going through some of the key questions on your Client Consultation form. You will want to find out how knowledgeable they are about home staging and what services they may want to hire you for. Many clients do not really know what home stagers have to offer so be prepared to let them know how many services you do offer for staging. Services do vary from stager to stager depending on what skills they have in their tool kit.

Even if a prospect has emailed you, it is far better sales technique to pick up the phone to follow up rather than to respond via email. This way, you immediately start building a rapport with the person. Once you are on the phone and the prospect is giving you a lot of positive signals that he or she would like to meet with you, stop talking and set up an appointment time.

Depending on the prospect's sense of urgency, suggest two options for meeting dates and times. If it is not quite so urgent, you may decide to make the appointment next week. **A word of caution:** Do not leave making the appointment for more than one week ahead. Many prospects, even though they say something is not urgent, still have a need and it is best to respond to that need in good time or someone else may! When you do make the appointment don't give the perception that you have no work scheduled so you can come any day. Rather, create the impression that you are busy and these are the two dates and times you have available. Ask the prospect which ones work for him or her. You can be flexible when you need to be to accommodate the other person's schedule and still be in control of the sales call.

During this qualifying call your prospect may ask what your services cost or, to put it more succinctly, "What do you charge?" If you are a new entrepreneur, you need to meet as many prospects as you can, so you do not want to quote a price. The reality is that you do not know what home staging services you will need to offer this prospect. The person may balk at your charges without having met you and really understanding how home staging can benefit him or her. In the beginning it is better to say, "Until I can determine what you need I really cannot quote you anything. By the time we have met and if you are interested in hiring me, I will provide you a quote based on the services you need. How does that sound?" This way you get to see if this is a good client for you, and he or she will get to know you more personally. Remember all the different emotions that come into play with the selling decisions the homeowner needs to make. Building a rapport will help ease the person's uneasiness.

Some of your prospects may say that another home stager will do a consultation for free. You need to decide if this is something you want to do or not. If you start doing consultations for free this will be expected of you all the time. It is natural for friends to tell other people what a home stager charged them if they are referring you, and they may very well say, "The consultation is free."

1.3 Consultation

At this point in the sales cycle, if you are actually meeting with the client, consider it a fairly good indication that he or she wants to do business with you. It is not always the case, but it is more often than not. Much has been discussed previously about conducting a home staging consultation in Chapter 10 so you may want to review that chapter. In this section some new points will be added and some key points will be repeated.

Now that you have an appointment set up and you are meeting with the prospect, you need to come across as the professional that you are. This means great grooming and professional dress. While you don't always know what your prospect will be wearing, you know the expression "It only takes a minute to make a good first impression" is so true. The prospect is deciding if he or she wants to do business with you or not — so dress the part!

Whenever possible, ask if you may take some *before* photos at the end of your consultation since this is usually when the home looks its worst (so all the better for your *after* photos).

The length of the call will depend on how much work the client needs and the time that has been allotted for the sales call. Most stagers make four hours the maximum time they will spend on one client call. Often you will be making recommendations if the call is more than one hour.

Refer back to your Client Consultation form for the questions you will ask. It is important to keep responding positively to what the clients' needs are because their needs are where their problem areas are. You are going to find solutions for them. Try trial closes such as, "It sounds like you do not know where to start?" Their response could be, "I am feeling overwhelmed." You might say in response, "I am here to give you a step-by-step plan so you know what you need to do, and where I can help. How does that sound?" Your soon-to-be-client may reply, "That sounds great. I'm breathing easier already!" Here you are building rapport and getting to the "yes, "which is what you need to close the sale.

If you have been referred by a realtor, make sure you have all the contact information you need on your Client Consultation form before you arrive. If this home has already been listed and is up on the Internet, take the time to look at the home and download some of the information from the site.

Keep in mind that your focus during your call is to help the client as much as possible in getting his or her property ready for selling. Even if the person seems overwhelmed and does not want to buy your services, treat him or her with respect and empathy. Selling a home is a very big job, especially if the client has lived in the home for a long time. Much emotion is attached to getting it ready for selling. The sales call is *all about the client* and not about you and how much you know about staging. Make the client feel good and assure him or her that the work is manageable!

During the consultation you will be taking a tour of the entire property to assess what needs to be done. Once you have done your walk about sit down with the client in a comfortable area to talk specifically about what needs to be done right away. This would include what you can do and what he or she needs to do to prepare the property for selling. As the person continues to warm up you are getting closer to making the final sale. This is where using your portfolio and telling stories of your successes will be appropriate.

1.4 Features and benefits

Once you have spent some time conversing with the client you will know if you have established a good rapport or not. Assuming you have, you can carry on with some small talk, making positive and genuine comments about the person's home. There has to be something good and appropriate you can tell the person about his or her home even if at first it does not seem so! The client may still need convincing that having his or her home staged is worth the time, money, and energy. By offering features and benefits you show and explain why home staging will improve his or her chances of selling for top dollar and in a quicker time than a home that is not staged.

During your sales call you will be discussing the features and benefits of your home staging services. This is an explanation of the terminology:

- **Feature:** *what* you are offering to the prospect (e.g., consultation, rearranging of furniture, decluttering, or recommendations).
- **Benefit:** *how* the prospect benefits (e.g., adding more market value to the

property, less stress involved, be more organized, etc.).

Make a list of some of the features and benefits your home staging company can offer.

1.5 Testimonials

To help support your sales call, client testimonials can be included in your sales presentations especially when you are offering your features and benefits or handling objections with your prospects.

Testimonials from your clients provide what is called *social proof* that you in fact are as fantastic as you claim to be! They give you credibility and speak volumes about your business. Your testimonials can be used for all sorts of marketing purposes such as on your website, business card, postcard or rack cards, flyers, and with the before-and-after photos in your portfolio or binder.

When you use someone's name in a testimonial it is best not to put in the person's last name unless it is a realtor who is fine with being associated with the home you have staged. You need to respect the privacy of your clients. Shorter testimonials are best and having a good variety of them will allow more people to connect with certain comments that would appeal to them.

Always ask for permission to take photos and use client testimonials. Use the Client Consent form (Form 2) as suggested in Chapter 10. If your client has not provided you with a testimonial within a two-week time period, write it through his or her eyes for the person and ask him or her to edit it.

The following are two testimonial examples:

"When *(name of home stager)* showed up with our realtor we didn't know what to expect. We had lived in our house for 30 years and we didn't know if we should paint everything

FEATURES AND BENEFITS OF HOME STAGING

Features — The What	Benefits — The How
You offer a multitude of staging services for the client to select from.	The client only uses and pays for those services he or she selects.
You use as many of the client's existing furnishings whenever possible.	This reduces the client's expenses so he or she doesn't need to spend any money on new furnishings.
You provide a professional, pulled together look for the client's target market.	The client's home looks and feels more harmonious. The home's best architectural features are highlighted.
You create new furniture, art, and accessory arrangements.	The client's home looks more spacious and will be staged with just the right amount of home decor items.
You focus on giving the home that WOW look.	Client can focus on what he or she needs to get done — personal things you cannot do.
You provide an objective and professional eye.	The client is coached on what things need to stay for the staging and what things can go.
If the client needs to make new purchases for the home, they will be the right ones and the home stager can get staging discounts.	For selling, the new purchases will be selected so that they will work in the client's new home too!
Home stager will provide a Recommendation Report.	A huge amount of stress is gone because the client will know exactly what needs to be done in the home, and when.
You take photos for the Internet listing.	The client and realtor have photos of the staged home looking its absolute best right after it is staged.

white or just leave it. Within one month *(name of home stager)* had turned our home into a showpiece! We rented some of her inventory and did what she told us to do. At the time it seemed like a lot of money but in the end it was so little compared to what we sold the house for!" Tim and Betty, Phoenix, AZ

"We are absolutely ecstatic with the staging job that *(name of home stager)* did for us. I never thought we would be able to get it all done but we did it. The Recommendation

Report was so helpful because we had the road map we needed. We did our part and *(name of home stager)* did his part and we sold in just three days!" Katie, Toronto, ON

1.6 Handling objections

In your sales calls you will meet both realtors and home sellers who are ready to hire you right away with no questions asked. You will also meet realtors and home sellers who have objections about using your services. If you are a new home stager, you may not be aware of some of the more common objections that realtors or home sellers might have. Following is a list of the typical staging objections that realtors and home sellers may present to you. If you review these often and learn the responses, in time you will be able to confidently handle any objection.

Handling staging objections from realtors:

✓ **Realtor objection:** "I don't want to pay for the staging services."

> **Home stager response:** "You don't have to pay for the staging services. In my experience, most realtors who pay my consultation look really great in their sellers' eyes. I can upsell my services once I meet the home seller. How does that sound?"

✓ **Realtor objection:** "I already use a home stager."

> **Home stager response:** "Brilliant, I would think you would! I have looked at your homes on the Internet and some of them look fantastic. I would like to present myself as your backup stager for times when your primary stager is not available. Would that make sense to you?"

Handling staging objections from home sellers:

✓ **Home sellers' objection:** "I don't know if I can afford this."

> **Home stager response:** "From my experience I know your home is one of the biggest investments in your life. Wouldn't you be willing to invest a small percentage of your future profit to make the most possible money you can? For a few thousand dollars you stand to make many

more thousands of dollars from selling quickly and for top dollar. Is this something that might appeal to you?"

Or

> **Home stager response:** "It seems to me it will be a lot less than your first price reduction. Wouldn't you agree?"

✓ **Home seller objection:** "My wife watches a lot of the decorating shows on television and she thinks we can do this ourselves."

> **Home stager response:** "I think you have done a nice job of your home for living. As a professional stager I know the trade secrets that make the house sell. How we live in our homes is definitely not how we sell our houses! I have an objective professional eye and I can get this done in far less time and with less energy than you would spend if you were doing it. I would think you have enough to do with the other chores of getting the house ready for selling. What do you think?"

Remember that if you have done a few staging jobs, even if they were for friends, you can still use this phrase, "in my experience." We all like to deal with people who have experience whether it is a hairdresser, carpenter, dentist, etc., so it makes sense that your potential clients like to deal with stagers who have experience.

1.7 Information Packages

There are a number of ways you can provide information about your services to your prospects. It may be as simple as giving your business card or postcard to someone you meet at a networking event. Or it may require an *information package*, which describes you and your company's services in more detail for a set appointment.

As you work in your business you will begin to learn which marketing materials to provide when and to whom. When you are providing information packages you will be incurring more expenses than just giving out your business card so it is important to determine which marketing materials are appropriate for which sales calls.

There are two types of packages of information that you can use in home staging: generic information package (with no rates) and specific bid or proposal package (with rates). Let's take a look at where you would use your generic or specific information package.

1.7a Generic information package

When you meet your prospect for the first time you always think in terms of *creating a great first impression* with your appearance. This holds true for any and all of your marketing materials. If you are doing a face-to-face meeting with a realtor, you are only meeting with the person because you want him or her to buy your services. This is a time when you may want to provide him or her with a generic information package.

If it is an office home staging talk, you might decide that using a file folder that prospects can put in their desk is the best way to go. Black is good and better yet, you can use a file folder in your brand color. Or you may decide that a glossy folder is how you would like to package it. If you get labels printed, you can put them on the front of a generic folder rather than using company folders. However you do it, make it look good!

If you are meeting with a prospective home seller, your generic information package would be suitable to leave with him or her along with your portfolio book. Again, this gives the person a few days to make his or her decision and for you to follow up.

In a generic information package you don't need to include your rates. You can make as many generic packages as you like since they will not contain your rates, which might need adjusting in the future. Having some packages already made will make your preparation for sales calls easier since they'll be ready to go.

You can work with a graphic designer to put some great packages together or do them yourself using a variety of software packages. See Form 10, which has also been included on the CD and you can customize the package to work for you.

Inside this generic information package you would include:

- A generic cover letter introducing yourself with your mission statement included — you do not need to put anyone's name on this unless you need to personalize it.

- A page of your services

- One or two pages of your best before and after photos along with testimonials or a separate testimonial page

- Business cards (always two)

- Postcards or rack cards

- A small giveaway with your branding on it such as a nail file, sticky notes, or pen (optional)

- Include any articles you have written or articles that promote home staging services if you don't have any of your own

Note: While color copying costs more than black and white copying, at least on your photos, spend the money on the color copies. They look so much better than just black and white.

FORM 10
GENERIC INFORMATION PACKAGE

Generic Information Package

For:
Real estate agents and home sellers looking to sell for top dollar by creating great first impressions — every time

Presented By:
(Insert your company name, address, phone number, website URL, and email address.)

*(**Note:** The above will be the only information on your title page for the document. Page 2 will include the following generic cover letter.)*

(Insert your company's name) — Home Staging Information Package

Thank you for this opportunity to provide you with *(insert your company's name)* Information Package.

Our goal is to work with real estate agents and home sellers to ensure that the property is target market ready, on budget, and on time for any home staging services that we provide. Included in our information package is our *Comprehensive Home Staging Services* list for your review. Many real estate agents and home sellers are unaware of everything that we can offer to increase the value of the property!

At the outset of our consultations many clients tell us that they are feeling overwhelmed and stressed because they had no idea what a big job lies ahead of them. That's where we come in. We take over and those feelings of being overwhelmed are replaced with a plan and action steps to get the house ready for its first showing. Agents also have peace of mind because they know we will deliver what we promise, and that means their clients are in good hands! In a recent study conducted by RESA® a recognized national real estate staging association, staged homes spent 78% less time on the market than unstaged homes.[*] And we all know what that means!

[*]**Note:** *If you have discovered your own statistics, use them; however, if you do need to use others' statistics, it is acceptable to use those of respected associations such as RESA.)*

(Insert your company's name) is flexible in our approach to home staging. We can do as little or as much, that fits within any budget whether working with just the home seller's furnishings or providing outside inventory to enhance the look of the home.

Feel free to contact me at any time with questions or concerns you may have.

Sincerely,

(Insert your name)
(Insert your title, for example, president)
(Insert your company's name)

(On the third and maybe even the fourth page, insert the before and after pictures of your previous home staging jobs.)

Recent Home Staging Projects

Using home seller's furnishings

(Insert before and after pictures of previous homes using the seller's furnishings.)

Using rental inventory

(Insert before and after pictures of previous homes using your company's or a rental company's furnishings.)

Client Testimonials

"Engaging *(insert your company's name)* to stage our house so that it was ready for the market was an investment that reaped huge benefits. For myself, *(insert your name)* reduced my stress levels to manageable levels (we were in the midst of an international relocation), suggested practical and affordable changes to our home, and knew which rentals to enhance the look of our home. A return visit from our real estate agent once the staging and decorating was complete, realized an increase in market value of $50,000. Our house sold within two weeks!"

(Client's first name only and city or town)

"I thought I knew what we needed to make our condo sell in today's market. My husband disagreed so we hired *(insert your company's name)* to see what changes he (or she) would recommend. Well I learned a lot and my choices were so off the mark! Our condo had multiple offers and I would always recommend hiring *(insert your name)* to anyone who is getting ready to sell. My color sense was fine for living but did not work for selling and *(insert your name)* knew that immediately. I like to live with way too much stuff and when we move I can get help again!"

(Client's first name only and city or town)

(Insert your company's name)
Comprehensive Home Staging Services List

We offer a variety of services to accommodate the needs of our varied clients. If you find that there are other services that you need for your home staging project, let us know!

Client Consultation: A client consultation can be very short, to help determine what needs to be done to stage the home. Or, it may be as long as four hours when specific recommendations are given to the client to help him or her prepare the property for selling.

Color Consultation: The majority of clients need a color consultation. We suggest colors that appeal to the majority of potential buyers. This may or may not be part of the initial consultation.

Report Recommendations: Many clients need a step-by-step plan to get them started on the right track. We can type a report for them or we can make recommendations to them room-by-room and they can do the report taking themselves. We make very detailed and specific recommendations in our reports.

Professional Organizing: Decluttering can be an overwhelming job for many clients. The longer they have lived in their homes the worse it can be. We offer this service to help them get started with what we call the "prepack." They have to pack up anyway; we just nudge them along in a good way!

Shopping: Someone has to do this and we are happy to step up to the plate and offer them our professional shopping services. We can shop for all their cosmetic home decor and minor renovation needs.

Sourcing for Rentals: Whether a client needs an entire vacant home of rental furnishings or just a few to update the look of the home for showing, we know the right sources to find the right product for each client.

Hands-on Installation/Staging: We offer the physical hands-on part of the actual *staging* of the home. We rearrange furniture, rehang art, attractively accessorize, create vignettes of interest that invite potential buyers in, and create the right look for every client's target market.

MLS (Multiple Listing Service) Photos: Once we have finished staging the home and it looks fabulous, we can email you our photos so you can use them on MLS or in any other marketing materials!

Move-in Services: We know what an exhausting job selling can be so we provide our clients with a special "move-in" service. We know how they like to live, so who better to set them up in their new home? We depersonalized their property for selling, now we can personalize their new home and usually in just one day!

Prices are quoted individually as each staging project is unique!

(On the final page you may want to include any published articles you have written or that are written by others about the home staging industry.)

1.7b Specific bid or proposal package

At some point in the selling cycle you will be asked to provide specific information with your rates to either the realtor or the home seller. This may happen when the prospective client wants to compare information to decide if he or she wants to go with home staging company A, B, or C. Or, there may not be someone else presenting or bidding at this time. Either way you would only provide your specific bid or proposal information with rates once you have gathered enough information during the consultation.

You may find that some home sellers or realtors want you to quote over the phone or just give them an estimate. As previously mentioned, it is not recommended that you quote them a price. You want to get in front of them to have the opportunity to make your presentation and actually see what you are bidding on! Remember that people buy from someone they know, like, and trust. This is not always the case and if someone is just looking for the cheapest price, you can usually tell. You can decide if you want that person as a client or not.

Your specific bid or proposal package would contain some or all of the same items that you have included in your home staging proposal estimate package or your generic information package. The main difference is that the specific bid would contain more information about you and your company, and be addressed to a specific person with a date included. You might even decide to present it in a more expensive folder than you generally do. Because, as you know, it is all about creating that great first impression, especially if there is potentially more work with this prospect. Once you know how you can meet the needs of your prospective client you can put realistic information together for your quote. It may or may not include some of your rental furnishings or some rental furnishings from a supplier.

1.8 Closing the sale

Once you have several trial closes working in your favor, you are ready to ask the client if he or she wants to hire you. When the client responds with "Yes, I want to hire you," the sale is technically ready to be *closed* by you saying with enthusiasm, "Great, I am ready to work with you!" You have now turned your prospect into your client.

The next step is to find out exactly when the clients want to proceed and what services they specifically want to hire you for. In some cases, you may need to discuss their homework with them and any other items of concern before the work gets underway.

If you are providing clients with strategic alliances, make sure they are aware that they need to contact them to schedule work. If you are offering this as a service, you will need to schedule and coordinate this for them. Of course, you would be charging for doing this coordination! (See Chapter 14 for more information on strategic alliances.)

1.9 Invoicing

You do not need to itemize every single thing on your invoice; instead, you can put a lump sum figure in the columns. However, be prepared to back up your totals with your own record keeping of each and every call you made in person, on the phone, and in emails. If you are offering rentals, you will need to know every single item that you are renting to ensure that when you do your destage every single item is accounted for. This applies to your own inventory and to any that you rented from a rental furnishing company.

If you do give any service free of charge for good will, make sure you indicate that on your invoice. It is always good for your customers to see that you did your open-house check-in at no charge (N/C) or complimentary to them. At times, clients may send you quite a few emails and phone you as they start their homework. If it amounts to more than 30 minutes of your time, it would be best if you charged for this.

Form 11 is a sample invoice for services. You may provide your own rental and delivery service so they might be separate services that you will bill for (see Form 12).

1.9a Types of payments

If you are just starting out, you need to decide what forms of payment you will take. In the beginning you may decide that cash or check works for you. However, over time it is best that you look into taking credit cards either online or offline. There are several different companies that offer merchant credit card services such as Moneris, First Data, and PayPal.

All major banks have credit card payment processing connections so it might be best to find out from your business bank what it has to offer you. Many associations will offer you member-discounted merchant credit card rates so check with groups that you have memberships with.

After you have done your research, if you find a particular company you like, but you are not happy with its rate, ask if they can offer you something lower and mention you are looking at other merchant account options. Go with the best overall deal for you and your business based on your needs.

1.9b Deposits

Some home stagers request the entire amount of their invoice to be paid at the close of the sale, some want a 50 percent deposit, and others want everything paid for up front except for the actual hands-on staging. The payment

for hands-on staging or installation would be required at the end of that day's work.

If you do have your credit card payments set up, it makes it very easy to put charges through once the sale is closed. Or, in the case of inventory rentals, you can put the next payment through on the first day of the second month without having to wait for a check to clear or having to collect cash from your client.

You can decide what will work best for you to ensure that you are always paid for the work you have done regardless of things moving ahead or not. It can and does happen that something prevents the home seller or realtor from moving forward with your services even though you have a signed contract. You do not want to be in a position in which you have not been paid for the work you have done. If you have done consultations, reports, shopping, and sourcing, you must be paid for what you've already done even if they put a "stop" on the staging project.

Some rental furnishing companies will require a deposit to hold the inventory especially if the company is busy, or it may request full payment up front for the first one-month rental period. You will need to ensure that you and your client completely understand any inventory rental terms.

1.10 Signing the agreement

If any rental inventory is involved, the clients will need to sign your Rental Inventory Agreement (see Form 13). In this agreement, they will be responsible for any damaged, lost, or stolen inventory and will be charged accordingly. Most agreements will request a replacement or damage fee based on the value of a product at a retail price. Even though you may get the product for a wholesale or

Staging Invoice

(Insert your company's name)
(Insert company's tagline)

Address:
Phone:
Email:
Website:

Bill To: **Invoice:** #555
First and Last Name: **Date:** mm/dd/year
Address:
City/Town, State/Province, Zip/Postal Code:

Date	Services Provided	Amount
mm/dd/year	**Services:** • Initial Consultation • Color Consultation • Shopping • Prepack/Organizing • Hands-on Home Staging	$2,500.00

Subtotal:	$2,500.00
TAX (at 5%):	125.00
TAX (at 5%):	125.00
TOTAL DUE:	**$2,750.00**

- 50% deposit is required to *(insert company's name)*
- Final payment is due on completion of the staging work.
- Make check payable to: *(insert company's name)*
- We accept Visa, MasterCard, and American Express

50% Deposit: $1,375.00

Thank you for your business.
We look forward to working with you again!

Staging Invoice

(Insert your company's name)
(Insert company's tagline)

Address:
Phone:
Email:
Website:

Bill To:
First and Last Name:
Address:
City/Town State/Province Zip/Postal Code:

Invoice: #444
Date: mm/dd/year

Date	Services Provided	Amount
mm/dd/year	**Monthly Rental Furnishings:** Upstairs • Master Bedroom • Guest Bedroom Main Floor • Living Room • Dining Room • Kitchen	$2,100.00
	Services: • Initial Consultation • Sourcing Rental Furnishings • Hands-on House Staging/Installation • Pack up of Rental Furnishings • Miscellaneous	$2,500.00
	Moving Costs: • Delivery, Pack up, and Return	$500.00

Subtotal:	$5,100.00
TAX (at 5%):	255.00
TAX (at 5%):	255.00
TOTAL DUE:	**$5,610.00**
50% Deposit:	$2,805.00

- 50% deposit is required to *(insert company's name)*
- Final payment is due on completion of the staging work.
- Make check payable to: *(insert company's name)*
- We accept Visa, MasterCard, and American Express

Thank you for your business.
We look forward to working with you again!

FORM 13
RENTAL INVENTORY AGREEMENT

TITLE

You agree that *(insert your company's name)* shall retain all right to ownership and title to any furnishing and accessory inventory provided. You also agree that no ownership or title of the furnishing and accessory inventory is transferred to you under this agreement, and you will not act or permit anyone else to do any act inconsistent with *(insert your company's name)* ownership and title of the inventory.

USE OF THE INVENTORY

You agree that the furnishing and accessory inventory will only be used at the designated address of *(insert home seller's address)* and only for the purpose for which the inventory has been intended. Subleasing or improper use of the inventory is strictly prohibited. Attached is a list of the inventory that you will be using.

RESPONSIBILITY FOR INVENTORY

You are responsible for the furnishing and accessory inventory from the time it is left on the property until the time it is returned to *(insert your company's name)*. If any inventory is damaged, stolen, and/or misused, the property owner agrees to reimburse *(insert your company's name)* for the full retail price.

CHARGES FOR INVENTORY

Your first invoice is for the first month's rental from *(insert date)* until *(insert date)*. Should you sell before that time period, the monthly billing still applies. Should you require the rentals for a second month, the same terms apply. From the third month onward you will receive 50% off of the original price.

Dated: *(insert month, day, and year)*

Signature: _____

Home Seller's Name: _____

Signature: _____
(Insert your name and your company's name)

*(**Note:** The Inventory List will be attached as a separate page to the agreement.)*

Inventory List for *(insert home seller's name)*

Room	Inventory	Quantity
Living Room	Art (large) Lamps Accessories Florals Black cushions	2 2 4 2 3
Kitchen	Table accessories Art (medium)	3 1
Hallway	Art (medium)	1
Master Bedroom	Bedding (king) Shams with pillows (queen) Accessories Florals Lamps Art (large)	1 4 3 2 2 1
Guest Bedroom	Bedding (king) Art (small) Florals Accessories	1 2 1 2
Bathroom	Art (small) Accessories	2 1

less-than-retail price you now have to spend time, money, and energy on replacing or repairing that piece of inventory.

You can also put all of your agreements into an All-in-One Rental Service Agreement, which you and your client both sign. You would make two copies of it. The agreement would contain:

- Request for permission to take photos
- Indication of the rates, terms, and conditions on your inventory
- A 24-hour cancellation policy
- Your service fees and any other necessary work not outlined in this agreement
- Overall agreement with all of the terms and conditions

You can use any of these Forms 11, 12, 13, and 14, together or separately and make any changes that meet the terms that suit you best. If you are renting inventory, you can decide what your terms are, and you can include discounts on a prorated weekly basis if that works best in your market.

FORM 14
ALL-IN-ONE RENTAL SERVICES AGREEMENT

BETWEEN

Client: _____

Address of property to be staged: _____

AND

Company: _____

Address: _____

SERVICE AGREEMENT

(Insert client's name) (hereinafter referred to as the "Client") is of the opinion that *(insert your company's name)* (hereinafter referred to as the "Company") has the necessary qualifications, experience, and abilities to provide services to the Client. The Company is agreeable to providing such services to the Client, on the terms and conditions as set out in this Agreement.

IN CONSIDERATION OF the matters described above and of the mutual benefits and obligations set forth in this Agreement, the receipt and sufficiency of which consideration is hereby acknowledged, the parties to this Agreement agree as follows:

ENGAGEMENT

1. The Client hereby agrees to engage the Company to provide the Client with services consisting of staging the property for sale, and such other services as may be agreed, and such other services as the Company may agree upon from time to time.

2. Staging, although proven to be effective, is a trained professional opinion and services provided do not in any way warrant the sale of a home.

3. Staging appointments canceled within 24 hours of the agreed-upon time will be charged a $ _____ rescheduling fee.

4. It is understood there are some risks involved in moving furniture and accessories as part of staging/redesigning services as contracted with the Company. Albeit rare to experience any damage, it is agreed by the Client to forgive small forms of damage.

5. There will be no future claim against the Company or any of their family, partners, associates, helpers, or employees for any injury to persons within the Client's property or damage or destruction of possessions or property belonging to the Client or others in and on the property.

6. It is warranted that the signer of this contract has the authority to authorize the movement of all furniture and accessories within the property.

7. Storage of unused items is the responsibility of the homeowner and may include a rental unit paid by the Client, or a designated area of the house.

8. All third-party involvement in preparing a home for sale is the responsibility of the homeowner. Any work performed by third-party companies recommended by the Company is not in any way the responsibility of the Company.

9. All pets should be removed from the property during services being rendered and it is not the responsibility of the Company to prevent pet escapes or injuries.

10. It is the sole responsibility of the Client to ensure driveways, walkways, and entrances are clear of any obstructions including snow, ice, mud, debris, etc., before the Company is able to commence services.

TERM OF AGREEMENT

The term of this Agreement will begin on the date of this Agreement and will remain in full force and effect until completion of the services. Both parties agree to do everything necessary to ensure that the terms of this Agreement take effect.

PHOTOGRAPHY AND PUBLICITY

The Client acknowledges that before and after photographs will be taken during the staging process and gives permission to the Company for use of these photographs in appropriate advertising and marketing materials.

PAYMENT EXPECTATIONS

For the services provided by the Company under this Agreement to begin work, a 50% (fifty percent) payment *(insert payment method such as MasterCard, Visa, cash, certified check)* is required and the remaining 50% (fifty percent) will be due no later than upon completion of the staging services. In the event the Client requests added services and/or product not included in the staging service, the Client agrees to compensate the Company for costs incurred and/or an hourly rate of $ _____.

The Client will pay to the Company compensation for the following:

1. Fee for full home staging services: $ _____

   This includes consultations, inventory rentals, pickup and delivery charges, home staging, and destaging.

2. Rental inventory first month fee: $ _____
   Rental inventory second month fee: $ _____
   Rental inventory third month fee (reduced by x%): $ _____
   Subsequent months fee (reduced by x%): $ _____

RENTAL POLICY

In the event the property does not sell within one month the **Rental Inventory Fee** will be as stated above per month thereafter and paid upon the next 30- (thirty) day date of each subsequent month. This Rental Policy will commence on the **signing date of this contract**. If the contract is canceled or the property is sold prior to the end of a month, the monthly rental fee specified above is still due and payable.

INVENTORY

1. Inventory remaining on the property will be listed on a separate document. Its replacement costs are the direct responsibility of the Client. All items are to be returned in the same condition as when placed; otherwise, retail replacement costs will be added to the invoice.

2. Certain personal inventory items are for display purposes only and not to be used, including all bedding, table linens, towels, etc. Inventory is not to be moved without written consent from the Company.

CONFIDENTIALITY

The obligation to protect the confidentiality of the Client's confidential information will survive the termination of this Agreement and will continue indefinitely.

The Company may disclose any of the confidential information to a third party where the Client has consented in writing to such disclosure.

INDEPENDENT CONTRACTOR

It is expressly agreed that the Company is acting as an independent contractor and not as an employee in providing the services hereunder. The Company and the Client acknowledge that this Agreement does not create a partnership or joint venture between them.

MODIFICATION OF AGREEMENT

Any amendment or modification of this Agreement or additional obligation assumed by either party in connection with this Agreement will only be binding if done in writing and signed by each party or an authorized representative for each party.

ENTIRE AGREEMENT

It is agreed that there is no representation, warranty, collateral agreement, or condition affecting this Agreement except as expressed in it.

SEVERABILITY

In the event that any of the provisions of this Agreement are held to be invalid or unenforceable in whole or in part, all other provisions will nevertheless continue to be valid and enforceable with the invalid or unenforceable parts severed from the remainder of this Agreement.

IN WITNESS WHEREOF the parties have duly executed this Rental Service Agreement dated this *(insert month, day, and year)*.

Client's Signature: _____
Print Name: _____

(Insert your company's name) Signature: _____
Print name *(person with signing authority)*: _____

1.11 Receiving final payment

If your payment terms have not included full payment up front, you need to indicate when final payment is due. For most stagers it makes sense that once the job is completed for the installation that payment should be made. It is most likely that you are contracting with other stagers so you will be expected to pay them when the work is done as well.

If you have to return to do the destaging and to pack up the inventory (whether yours or from a rental furnishing company), make sure you charge for this as well. Most stagers do estimate the amount of time it will take them to pack based on how long it took them to stage and/or install the inventory, and get payment for this when they do the staging or installation.

2. Follow-up

Follow-up is one of the areas where the majority of home stagers (and many other business people) neglect, and lose business as a result. The importance of good follow-up cannot be stressed enough.

Even in the beginning if you do not have separate database software, at the very least put your client information in an Excel spreadsheet containing all of their contact information. At some point you will be able to purchase more expensive software to track your client database.

As mentioned in Chapter 8, you might consider using an electronic greeting card system such as SendOutCards that allows you to personalize your cards with your before-and-after photos or choose from the thousands they have in their system. This is a nice soft-sell way of keeping in touch by sending out cards on special days or every few months to let clients know about some special offer that you have, or to say a simple "hello" to them.

If you have made up a small giveaway with some kind of branding on it, it can be a nice thing to leave behind once you have finished your work with the client. Some stagers get candles or soaps made up with their branding on them. In the beginning this may be too costly, but be creative and think of what you could leave behind that would be memorable.

Once you are up and running and doing your monthly (to start) then bimonthly or weekly e-newsletter or ezine, you can keep in touch with your clients by offering tips and information of value to your clients. Remember once your clients get to know you, like you, and trust you, they will be more interested in what you are doing.

There are many ways to say "thank you" to your clients — be creative and do something memorable for them. As has already been mentioned and is worth repeating, your home staging business is going to grow by referrals and repeat clients. If you are in regular contact with your clients, it is likely they will refer you or use your services again.

Remember to keep checking the Internet posting to see if your client's property has sold. You can also follow up with either the realtor or the home seller to see how things are going. If you do have inventory in the client's home, you will need to check at the end of each month if the property is still on the market.

If you really want to take the approach of being their "home staging coach," checking in more frequently would be worthwhile!

13
Hiring Contractors versus Hiring Employees

The start-up phase of your business is a fun and creative time; it is very empowering to be running your very own business. However, over time you may find that you do not have all the necessary skill sets to move your business forward.

When you are starting out you will need to have someone work with you for the actual physical home staging. Most home stagers find someone qualified to contract with in the beginning. It is not necessary to hire employees since the physical work is carried out per project and not on a daily basis.

With your plan in place it will only be a matter of time until you are in a position to hire contractors or employees on a more regular basis. Whether you are working with a contractor or an employee, remember that the person represents your company. Only work with people who represent your brand in the best possible light. It is your company's reputation that goes along with anyone you work with or refer people to.

Consider looking at some of the areas that you are not so strong in and delegate that work. Some areas might include but are not limited to the following:

- Hands-on staging
- Graphic design
- Website development
- Bookkeeping and accounting
- Administration

For each of these areas you need to look at the skill set that is required so you find the best fit, at the best price.

On occasion you may need to hire a professional contractor to do one-time-only project work for you such as a lawyer or trademark specialist. Ask people you trust for referrals.

1. Home Staging Contractors

Since the first person you will most likely contract with is someone to help you with the hands-on home staging, let's take a closer look at the pros and cons of using contractors versus hiring employees for your hands-on home staging jobs.

You may need someone to assist you with some aspects of hands-on home staging or move-ins if you offer these services. Typically you will only need to have someone work with you when you are physically moving furniture, hanging art, or any other associated physical tasks with the onsite staging, destaging, and move-ins. You will be able to conduct the majority of your other service offerings on your own, which means all the revenues go directly to you and your company.

Skill levels for assistants and contractors vary in the industry. Some people will contract someone just to do the physical work and he or she will not be required to provide much input to the creative part of the staging work. Other people will train an assistant by showing and explaining to him or her the basic skills needed to do the work. You can pay this contractor minimum wage or determine an amount that is agreeable to both parties.

Some stagers do like to bring an assistant or team member with them during consultations so they can strategize about what needs to be done in the home and how they will do it. One team member may also be better skilled in

a certain area (such as color selection) than the other. This scenario happens more often when two stagers "partner up" and work together.

The majority of home staging companies hire contractors so that they do not have to incur the employee costs associated with hiring someone. A contractor is someone who has his or her own business and who works for someone else on an as-needed basis.

The contractor is responsible for providing the home stager with an invoice indicating his or her "fee for services." The home stager pays the contractor and this payment becomes an expense that the home stager deducts for income tax purposes. Technically, the contractor should come to the home staging job with his or her own tools.

You need to check your insurance contract to see if it stipulates that any contractor working with you also needs to have his or her own insurance, for any of your claims to be valid when working with a contractor. You might want to check out information specific to your city or state or province for a better understanding of what constitutes a contractor in your area.

Note: On occasion the homeowner may help you and if so, the person needs to be aware that he or she is responsible for any damage that might occur while doing the home staging tasks. If the homeowner wants to help you with your staging job, do not lower your rates since the person cannot get the result he or she wants without you doing the work and directing. If the homeowner does help you with preparing the house for selling, he or she must have his or her own insurance coverage.

1.1 Pay rates for home staging contractors

There is no governing body that dictates what rates you need to pay your contractors or your employees. From the research gathered for this book, and from my years of experience teaching in metropolitan cities and smaller towns, the range of pay rates provided appear to be consistent in the home staging business throughout North America.

Many stagers base their rate to pay contractors on the skill levels of assistants or contractors. It would make sense that if you decide you will contract with someone just to do the physical work and not request much input to the creative part of the staging work, then the person would be paid your lower contract rate.

If someone you contract with has been professionally trained, he or she can offer more than someone who has not been trained. It would make sense to pay the trained person more. Often home stagers find a few good stagers to work with and eventually team up with the one or two contractors because they work really well together.

Here are some guidelines that you can use to determine what to pay your contractors. (Remember though, you need to find what is an equitable pay rate in your market.)

- ✔ **Untrained assistants and contractors:** Require slightly higher than minimum wage or in urban areas $10 to $12 per hour (may vary in your market).

- ✔ **Trained assistants and contractors:** In urban areas the pay may be $15 to $20+ per hour or 20 percent of the revenues for the work done for you or with you.

- ✔ **Exclusive special contractors:** These contractors are the ones you will work with most often, and you will work with them when they need a contractor. The pay for these types of contractors is 50 percent of the revenues for the work done for you or with you.

- ✔ **Partner assistant:** This type of assistant and you will split 50/50 for hands-on staging.

- ✔ **Friend or partner:** You decide what you want to pay the person.

Some stagers will contact other stagers to let them know they would like them to work with them on a staging job. The average industry standard to pay a fellow stager is 20 percent of the hands-on job charges. It bears repeating that you need to determine an equitable contractor pay rate based on what is fair market value in your area. It may be much less than 20 percent of what you charge the client, or much higher.

1.2 Qualifications of home staging contractors

One of the most important areas to look at when contracting with another home stager is that you both get along and work well together. If you need to train someone, the best way is to let the person job shadow you to see what you do. If you have a system set up for doing each room, your trainee should be able to follow what you do quite easily.

Here are a few characteristics to look for in a contractor:

- ✔ Reliable
- ✔ Hard working
- ✔ Punctual
- ✔ Ability to follow instructions
- ✔ Ability to make good decisions
- ✔ Ability to problem solve creatively
- ✔ Good design and style skills
- ✔ Willingness to do whatever it takes to get the job done

You may want to have a dress code of your branding colors, or get t-shirts and/or vests made with your logo on them. That way the team looks professional at all times, and every person working with or for you is making a good impression about your company.

2. Home Staging Employees

In the start-up phase of your home staging business it is not likely that you will be hiring any employees. You might decide this is definitely in your business plan in the future, especially if you have your own inventory and need to track that on an ongoing basis. When you are ready to hire an employee make sure your business is steady and decide whether you are going to hire the person part time or full time.

Most home stagers do not start out with employees unless they have a retail space that requires someone work there on a daily basis. Home stagers that have a store location and not a home office may also rent inventory to the public and other home stagers. Some stagers who do rent out their own inventory also provide home staging services. They may contract with someone to be available to show a home stager their inventory but it is unlikely it would be done on a daily basis.

When you are looking for employees you will need to have a good job description prepared and go through an interview process to find the best candidate to work for you. You will need to prepare legal agreements appropriate to your state or province for hiring and firing scenarios.

2.1 Pay rates for employees

Advice on pay rates for employees is somewhat more challenging to offer. The best way to figure it out is to contact your local employment office or ask other people who have hired for similar types of positions what they pay their employees.

If you hire employees, you need to pay all the associated costs and make the appropriate tax deductions. Labor and employment laws differ throughout North America. You need to ensure you are following the laws and complying with the rules and regulations your state or province sets forth.

When you are hiring you need to take into consideration all of the following additional costs associated with part-time or full-time employees:

- Vacation pay
- Employer taxes — Federal Insurance Contributions Act (FICA) in the United States and Canada Pension Plan (CPP) in Canada
- Sick leave
- Maternity or parental leave
- Workers' compensation
- Hours of work including breaks
- Statutory holiday pay
- Bonding costs

As an employer you also need to notify your tax department so you can remit the appropriate tax deductions. Regardless of who is doing your bookkeeping you need to be aware of what legal requirements you will have to follow for the Internal Revenue Service (IRS) in the United States, and the Canada Revenue Agency (CRA) in Canada.

Information about payroll and payments that you need to make can be found in the United States through the IRS and in Canada through CRA.

3. Other Considerations When Hiring Contractors or Employees

There are a few other areas to take into consideration when finding someone to work with you, whether it is a contractor or an employee. When hiring someone it is not just the costs that you need to consider but also your time and energy!

Take a look at this list before you begin hiring employees or contractors:

- ✓ Where will you find them?

- ✓ How will you find them?

- ✓ Have you created a job description so they understand what is required and the qualifications needed to do the work?

- ✓ Do you have an application for them to complete?

- ✓ How much time will it take to find them?

- ✓ How much time will it take to interview and hire them?

- ✓ How much time will it take you to do reference checks?

- ✓ How much training is needed and do you need to provide training?

- ✓ What new overhead costs will you have?

- ✓ Who will draw up the contract for hiring?

- ✓ What happens if it does not work out (i.e., do you have a probationary time period or a termination policy in place)?

Make a list of the positions you need to fill. Create a skill set checklist and indicate what the cost would be for working with a contractor versus hiring an employee.

14
Building Strategic Alliances

In Chapter 3 we discussed your target market and how home sellers and real estate agents are your two primary targets. A secondary target for you is your *strategic alliances*. As you start to think about growing your business you will soon realize that you need good strategic alliances that you can refer your clients to, to do the necessary work needed to prepare a property for selling. It is critical that you have great relationships with anyone that you recommend to your clients. You may find that many of your strategic alliances will offer you referrals or commissions which can be another revenue stream for your home staging business.

According to Wikipedia the definition for a strategic alliance is:

A formal relationship between two or more parties to pursue a set of agreed upon goals or to meet a critical business need while remaining independent organizations.

Since most home stagers are solo-entrepreneurs who hire contractors it would make sense that you have a ready and reliable source of strategic alliances to call on and refer to your clients when needed. It is critical that you build great relationships with your alliances so that you can communicate when things are going well, and especially when things are not going well. Most home stagers will agree that certain tradespeople can have great intentions but they do not always deliver the required results in the time frame stated, and often go over budget. It will be up to you to follow up and check on the quality of work your strategic alliances are delivering during the project, and when it's completed.

1. Identifying Your Strategic Alliances

Many new home stagers say they do not have any strategic alliances and are at a loss as to where to find them. Have no fear, because they are everywhere and you probably already have some you were not aware of! For example, think about whom you have hired or a family member has hired as a painter, contractor, gardener, handyperson, or an electrician. Ask the family member if he or she liked working with the person and if the person delivered what he or she promised on time and within budget. Over time you will be able to build up your strategic alliances so you can confidently refer them to your clients.

Another great way to build your strategic alliance list is by finding out who your clients have used in the past that they were happy with. Every time you meet someone new, at a networking event, or when you see a potential alliance's truck parked outside a home, introduce yourself and see if you have a connection with him or her. If you do, then take the person's business card and follow up with him or her so you can decide if the two of you can work together. You refer the person, and he or she refers you. Ask the potential alliance if he or she pays referral fees if you find business for him or her. You might also consider offering referral fees to some of your best strategic alliances.

Many tradespeople leave their business cards in coffee shops or hardware stores. Take the information and follow up and see if you want to work with them. You can also check out the classifieds in local newspapers as tradespeople often advertise in newspapers.

It is best to have at least three strategic alliances for each category where you think you may be referring someone to your clients. You will need to have more painters and small handyperson alliances than any other as they are often booked up, especially in summer months. If you live in an area that has a really

warm climate, summer may in fact not be your painter's prime time of business. Check it out and make sure you have more than enough painters for your busy home staging season.

Following is a list of most of the strategic alliances that you will need to help build your business.

- Realtors
- Mortgage brokers
- Appraisers
- Inspectors
- Builders
- Painters
- Handypersons
- Renovators
- Electricians
- Contractors
- Closet-making companies
- House cleaners
- Window cleaners
- Carpet cleaners
- Flooring companies
- Window treatment suppliers
- Glass and door companies
- Equipment rental stores for pressure washers, etc.
- Kitchen and bath stores
- Boutique home decor stores
- Lighting stores
- Landscapers
- Paving companies

- Moving companies
- Portable on demand storage (PODS)

On the CD you will find a Strategic Alliance List that you can use to compile your list of strategic alliances and their contact information.

2. Disclaimer for Strategic Alliances

It's best to put a disclaimer in your list of strategic alliances stating something similar to the following:

Our company has either personally used the services of our preferred strategic alliances, or our clients have referred them to us stating they were reliable and provided a quality service for them. Each strategic alliance has his or her own business and is responsible for his or her own insurance, quotes, and services provided to you.

3. Discounts and Referral Fees from Strategic Alliances

Most of the suppliers that you source from should give you a discount starting at 10 percent. The more you purchase from them, or refer business to them, the higher the discount can become. Typically you just need to show that you have an established business and complete an application form for these. Many small companies starting out will be asked to pay by credit card at the time of purchase. Once they become more established, and if they operate with very large purchases, they may be invited to set up an account with suppliers so they can bill monthly.

Always ask your suppliers if they give discounts to stagers — they almost always will but only if you ask!

You may also find that some of your strategic alliances will not give you a monetary option but would rather work out an arrangement whereby you refer them to your clients and they refer you to their clients. The better relationship you have, and the more referrals you can give a strategic alliance, the more likely both businesses will grow and prosper.

3.1 Marking up products

If you have wholesale suppliers in your area, it is worth meeting with them to see what form of discount you can receive. Many furniture wholesalers and suppliers of fabrics and window treatments will give you a sizeable discount compared to what you may receive from a retail store. Some wholesalers will not deal directly with the public and only with tradespeople, whereas others will deal directly with the public.

With some industries you will be getting a 50 percent wholesale discount. Many stagers like to mark up this price by 25 percent so that they can tell their clients they, as a professional stager, got them 25 percent off the product purchase. It is entirely up to you what arrangement you make.

Something that is important to decide is who will be making the initial purchase. If you do, you can give your client an invoice with the 25 percent added. Make sure you know if there are any extra charges such as delivery.

If something is being custom-made, find out what the return policies are for that (if returns are even allowed). If you have paid for it, you may not be able to get out of it so check the terms and policies of the wholesalers very carefully.

4. Joint Ventures

Some people mistake a joint venture for a strategic alliance. A joint venture is "a legal entity formed between two or more parties to undertake an economic activity together." The joint venture could be a one-time project or an ongoing project. All or both parties would be responsible for selling and marketing or agreeing to who sells and markets the joint venture.

Since this book is for you, the start-up home staging entrepreneur, it is unlikely that in your first few months or even first year that you will be undertaking a joint venture with someone else. Keep in mind for future business growth once you are well established that you may want to consider joint ventures (or not).

15
Bookkeeping and Invoicing

It is most likely when you are starting up your home staging business that you will not be contracting out your bookkeeping. Most small-business entrepreneurs do their own bookkeeping for a few years because they can handle the amount of receipts and record keeping that they need to do. However, there isn't any rule that says you can't hire a bookkeeper right away, especially if you are incompetent in this area! It is one of the more critical areas in business that you need to keep records of — this is a time when "more is better." That means keeping all your receipts for *anything* that is business related — from the smallest dollar store purchase to bigger items such as a furnishings inventory.

1. Setting up Your Business Bank Account

If you are starting out as a sole proprietorship, your bookkeeping will be less complicated than if you are starting out by incorporating. As a

sole proprietor you can do your business banking in your own personal checking account, but if you really want to project the image of being in business and keep things straight is best that you set up a business bank account.

In order to set up a business bank account you will need proof that you are a registered and legitimate business. When you go to the bank bring along your business registration number form, proof of business incorporation (if you have gone this route), and government-issued photo identification to start the process. You will be given the option of certain types of checks along with the type of book you can keep your checks in. It's entirely up to you how fancy you want to get or if you just want to stick with the basics. You will also receive a deposit receipt book which is a great idea if you are only taking cash and checks in the beginning. This allows you to keep track of your incoming revenues.

At the end of each month you will receive your bank statement along with copies or print-outs of the checks you have written. You will then need to compile a bank reconciliation statement for your own records and for your year-end reports whether you are filing them yourself or giving them to a bookkeeper or an accountant.

If you have incorporated, you need to use a bookkeeper and an accountant and file more often than a sole proprietor. Check with your accountant as to when and how you need to do your business banking along with your tax filing.

2. Bookkeeping and Filing

In Chapter 9, Exercise 16, we took a look at setting up a worksheet so that you could start recording your expenses versus your income on a monthly basis.

At the beginning of my business I did not know how to use Excel so I did my record keeping manually in a Word document! Over time, I eventually hired a bookkeeper and accountant, to whom I now enjoy delegating all of the bookkeeping!

2.1 Software packages

There are several good software packages to choose from for your bookkeeping needs. QuickBooks and Simply Accounting are the two most commonly used for smaller start-up businesses. If you are computer savvy, you can buy the product and install it yourself and set up your system. If you are not computer savvy, it is recommended that you hire a bookkeeper to install the software and to give you some basic training.

2.2 Bookkeepers

If you are in a position to afford a bookkeeper, ask people in your networking groups who

they are using. You could do an online search for bookkeepers but make sure you check their credentials when you interview them. This is an area that you cannot afford to make mistakes in especially should you be audited at some future time.

Decide what kind of arrangement you will make with your bookkeeper. For instance, will you file everything in an indexed file folder and give this to your bookkeeper monthly to do your statements? Or will you give your bookkeeper your monthly receipts and let him or her put them in the file folders and prepare the monthly statements? Do you want your bookkeeper to prepare your year end as well or will you take this to an accountant for tax purposes?

2.3 Accountants

When you are first starting your business you may decide to meet with an accountant to determine if you are going to establish yourself as a sole proprietor or incorporate your business. Or you may have decided already what you wanted to do.

It is always best to get the advice of professionals if you are not sure about something in your business. It is best to be aware of the legalities in the beginning rather than finding out later that you didn't do something right.

Many stagers only use an accountant to prepare their year-end taxes. You do not need to hire an accountant to keep your books. If you do, you will be paying more than you would for a bookkeeper who has the skills you need to keep your books.

2.4 Filing systems

It is wise to set up your filing system from day one of your business. A simple way is to use an accordion file folder and file your clients' information alphabetically. You can record all the time that you spend with your client and the charge for services with the Client Consultation (Form 1) mentioned in Chapter 10.

Your record keeping of charges you'll need to bill would look something like Sample 8.

You would transfer the charges to your invoice and take the invoice with you when you are doing the work, or email it, or mail it to your client. Most stagers starting out collect payment at the time of the work or take a deposit if there will be some time in between. Some stagers request the total payment before they do any work so they are assured of being paid and not having to wait to collect their hard-earned money!

3. Forms of Payment

Small businesses have a few options for how to receive payment for their services.

3.1 Cash or check payment

When you are just starting out you may be set up to take only cash and check payments. This is an acceptable way to start your business. Depending on the type of bank account you set up, cash and checks will cost a nominal amount to deposit compared to the fees associated with a merchant account system.

3.2 Credit card payments

Setting up a merchant account credit and debit card system gives the impression of being a more established business. Like most of the suggestions being made in this book, you are asked to check out at least three different suppliers for many of your business needs. Finding a merchant credit and debit card supplier is no different. Many business owners will apply for this type of account through their existing business banking partner. Many chambers of commerce, boards of trade, and professional networking groups have discounts for their members. Ask around to get the best price for the best service.

Remember that while this is a cost to you, you really do need to spend money to make money in any business. If your clients prefer to pay with credit cards, it is worth the charges you will incur. Most people will pay on the spot with a credit card versus cash or check.

The rate that you are charged by your supplier will vary based on a variety of things such as your credit rating, the length of time you have been in business, and whether or not your clients sign their credit slips or you take the information over the phone. Do your research to get the best rate and find the most convenient way to take and process payments.

SAMPLE 8
RECORD KEEPING

Date	Service	Hours/Charge	Invoice Amount	Invoiced
11/23/2011	Consultation	3.5 hours @ $100	$350 plus tax	✓
12/13/2011	Hands-on staging	6 hours	$800 plus tax	✓
12/15/2011	Open house check in	Complimentary	N/C	

If you are renting inventory on a monthly basis, it is great to be able to process the next month's revenues with the credit card rather than having to get another check, unless of course, you have gotten postdated checks from your client.

3.3 Internet and online banking

There are more and more banking services being offered online now. Check with your banking institution to see what type of payment system you can set up for clients wanting to pay directly to your bank account. Money can be transferred from your client's account to your bank account electronically.

You might also want to consider researching the cost of setting up a system such as PayPal or 1ShoppingCart. These services often cost more but can be more convenient than processing credit card payments through your merchant account with your bank. If you were planning on having a lot of inventory, either of these payment methods would make sense.

16
Your Home Office

As a home stager there is no reason to have a retail store location unless you are providing other services that would warrant the need for a storefront. This could be the case if you are offering services as part of a design store or home decor store. However, you may have a warehouse in which you keep your inventory and it would make sense to have a desk there. You may or may not have your computer (desk or laptop) at your warehouse location but you would most likely have your cell phone with you.

1. Setting Up Your Home Office

The following sections discuss what you will need to do to set up your home office.

1.1 Home phone

If you live by yourself, change the phone message to indicate that the caller has reached the "home office of *(your name)*" and that you will return the call promptly. However, if you have

family, you need to set up a phone messaging system that allows your callers to select the prompt that will direct them to your business, so that they may leave a message in your caller box. You will need to check with your phone company to find out which is the best package for you.

One of the worst scenarios is when a potential client or client phones and someone in the family answers the phone in a very unprofessional manner. It is going to leave your caller wondering if he or she has the right number or, and worse yet, he or she may look elsewhere. You may have to train your family to understand that you are using your phone for business now.

1.2 Cell phone

There is an abundance of wireless phones that you can now choose from. You may decide to start with just a cell phone and move up to a

BlackBerry or an iPhone so that you can also receive your emails and have Internet access if you feel you need that. Research at least three phone plans to find the best deal and services that you will need. Only buy what you need as phone companies typically try and sell you much more than you require to be efficient in your business dealings via a cell phone.

Again, because your prospects or clients will be calling you on this phone, make sure you have a professional message on it.

1.3 Toll-free numbers

Some home stagers like to project the perception that they are a bigger company than they are. If you think you will be able to provide services outside your area, or if you have home stagers you know you could contract within other areas of the country, a toll-free line might be a good idea.

Toll-free numbers are relatively inexpensive to purchase. Do an Internet search and find out which the best service provider is in your area. You can get your toll-free calls to come directly to your phone or your computer.

1.4 Computers and software packages

It doesn't matter whether you use a laptop or a desktop computer for your business. What will be important is to have all your files on one computer for easy access. There are lots of deals out there on computers and the prices are being reduced daily so find the best one for your needs at this time.

It is highly recommended that you let the family know that it is your business computer and they are not to use it. There have been horror stories of children using someone's computer only to find that viruses had been downloaded which crashed the computer. The repairs for this can be costly and, even worse, your files and photos can be in danger.

You should have the latest software packages on your computer such as a word processing package, with spreadsheet appliations and graphics. In the beginning, you may be doing all of your administrative work so the more packages you have the better. There are many free courses being offered for start-up entrepreneurs so do some research in your area and see if you can get some free training or low-cost training to help you in the beginning.

Your email program can be used for not only sending and receiving emails but you can put your tasks and follow-ups in it and work with the calendar to schedule your appointments. Get your graphics person to create an e-signature for you and/or e-stationery for your outgoing emails. It adds another memorable marketing piece to your brand.

Adobe Photoshop is a good picture software to have for organizing all the photos you will be taking. It is easy to manipulate for uploading photos to your website, blog, and for articles for which you supply photos.

1.5 Desk setup

You might not start out with your dream-office setup so focus on the essentials to get you started. The style and shape of your desk may depend on how much space you have for your office. If you have a small space, consider getting a desk wardrobe that allows you to close the front doors so that it looks more presentable when you are not using it, and takes up less space.

Regardless of where you set up your office, even if it is a corner of a room, let everyone know this is your office and that they should not touch anything in that area. It's not recommended that you set up a desk in your bedroom as the bedroom needs to be kept for sleeping and relaxation, and not a reminder of all the work you have to do! Some home stagers have even been able to set up a desk in a big closet that was not being used. Think outside the box and make it your space!

For income tax purposes technically you are supposed to have a *dedicated* home office space that is not a part of a bedroom, living room, or dining room. However, if you have sectioned off part of a room it should be acceptable as a tax deductible business item. Check with your tax authority on this one.

2. Professionalism at Home

One of the most important concepts for you to understand when you are setting up your home office is that you are a *professional* home stager now. Your friends and family need to know that you are setting up rules so that they respect the boundaries of your new office and your time. You must do your part in changing the thinking in *your* mind as well so you see yourself in this new role!

Now that you are a professional home stager, you need to start acting the part even when you are at home, and especially when you are out and about. Many people seeking to become home stagers have played other roles in their lives before they decided to enter this new profession. It is really important that *you* get the message out there with every single contact you make that you are a professional home stager now — act like it! This is part of the parcel of your brand now!

2.1 Dress the part

Regardless of how much time you are going to spend in your home office or out meeting prospects and clients, you need to dress the part. Obviously you don't need to be as dressed up at home compared to how you would look meeting a prospect or client. However, if you sit down at your computer in your pajamas or

sweats, you will be in a very relaxed mood and it is most likely that this will be translated into the work you do for that day. What would you do if a prospect or client called and wanted to see you in one hour? It might be a missed opportunity!

Perhaps you have young children and you can only find a few hours in the day to get to your computer. The same rule applies. Take some time to groom yourself so you put your professional hat on. It makes a world of difference with how you feel about yourself if you take the time to get in the right mind set. People around you will start responding differently to you but you need to make the change.

2.2 Set office hours

You determine your office hours. In the beginning, if your schedule permits, you may start out by making yourself available 24 hours a day, seven days a week. Or, you might only be able to work on weekends or at night if you have other obligations in the beginning. You need to decide what will work best for you.

If you do have other obligations, perhaps another part-time job or taking care of children, you can take control and let your prospects or clients know that you have only specified times that you are available so that they get the impression that you are really busy.

Successful time management means you need to control what your work week looks like. When you set up your work week, if you have other obligations, block them off in your calendar and suggest times that you are available and book your appointments during those times. This way you control your schedule and you don't become so frazzled trying to do it all.

Let family and friends know what your work hours and days are. This will take some time and adjustment for everyone. Put a sign on your office door (if you have one) that lets the family know you are "in" or "out" of your office. When you are *out* of the office, dedicate that time to your family and friends. When you are *in* your office, focus only on office-related work and not personal. By setting up systems like this you will be far more productive and respectful of yourself as a new home staging professional. Give it a try because it really does work!

3. Getting Rid of the Home-Office Blues

Once in awhile you may feel like nothing is happening and you may even have some negative mind traps going on. The best way to get over these home-office blues is to get out and get connected to other positive professionals. Get networking!

You might also want to consider being part of a "mastermind" group or any association with like-minded and forward-thinking business entrepreneurs such as real estate staging professionals.

Another person to consider having around is your business coach. I have mentored hundreds of women over the years and I know for a fact that the time we have spent together has propelled them forward in their businesses much faster than if we had not been working together!

If you are really feeling isolated and overwhelmed in your business, it is okay once in a while to just take a break from your work and take some "me" time. The great advantage of being an entrepreneurial home stager is that you can set your work schedule and make up for lost productive hours another time.

17
The Stage Is Set

What an exciting time for you! With what you already know about yourself and with all of the information in this book about how to start and run your home staging business, you are ready to get on with your new life as a home stager!

If you haven't done all the exercises in this book (and included on the CD), go back and do them now. They will offer more insight into who you are and what you want your new business to look like.

You might not have been born an entrepreneur yet with knowing what you want, the desire to succeed, and the belief in yourself, these three things will get you through the ups and downs of your new business.

As you start and grow your business you will definitely be changing the way you do some things to make your systems more efficient and to manage your time, money, and energy better. The most important thing for

you to know is that you can do this if you follow the information provided in this book.

1. Celebrating Your Successes

All entrepreneurs need to take time to celebrate every single success they have. It can be the smallest to the biggest of accomplishments — the size does not matter — so acknowledge your achievements in everything.

This is a way for you to stay positive and move forward. Try giving yourself a high five if no one else is around for you to high five! You might want to treat yourself to something really special to mark your most significant accomplishments.

2. Working with Affirmations

In today's world we hear a lot about how powerful affirmations can be, especially to counter negative self-talk. Find some affirmations that speak to you and put them where you can see them so you set the tone of your day feeling good about yourself.

There are thousands of self-help and self-growth blogs and books that are available to you for free and online. You might even want to subscribe to a free "daily affirmation" from a website.

Know that every business, large or small, has its ups and downs during the business cycle. Positive affirmations will keep you up when those down times come around (which too shall pass).

3. Get Connected

Most home staging schools require that you take their courses to become eligible to be a member of their association or organization. They offer credentials and designations to their graduates and members. By being a member, you have the opportunity to stay connected through forums, blogs, teleseminars, workshops, members-only sites, meetings, and conferences.

In my school you earn your Professional Real Estate Staging (PRES®) designation. PRES members have access to a PRES members-only site where they can connect with each other, offer advice, and share opinions. Consider signing up for free ezines with PRES or other staging schools if they are offered. That way you get the latest information in home staging and fantastic tips on how to run your home staging business. Do some Internet searches to see what is available to you for future ongoing learning.

Another option for you to get connected is to become a member of the Real Estate Staging Association (RESA®) as this organization is comprised of home stagers in North America. RESA provides any industry-related professional, regardless of his or her training, the opportunity to get connected with other home staging professionals. You may even meet colleagues who live in the same area as you, so you might have the opportunity to work together as contractors for each other.

4. Working with Coaches or Mentors

Being in business by yourself can seem overwhelming at times, especially in the start-up phase. Most successful home stagers have worked with a coach or mentor at some point in their business life. It is a proven fact that entrepreneurs who hire a coach or mentor succeed 50 percent more in business than those who did not make the investment of time, money, and energy.

Look for coaches and mentors who have worked with other home stagers, or ask other home stagers who they would recommend. Finding the right fit for you will be paramount in your success. Coaches keep you focused on your goals when you get sidetracked or uncertain as to what to do next. Coaches and mentors are your cheerleaders who are always there to support you in your new and fabulous business of home staging!

Surround yourself with people who support you in this new venture — you deserve it!

If you are interested in working with me as your mentor or coach check out www.EmpoweredWomenInBusiness.com. I would love to work with you if we are a good fit.